The Twentieth Century Pulpit

VOLUME II

The Twentieth Century Pulpit

VOLUME II

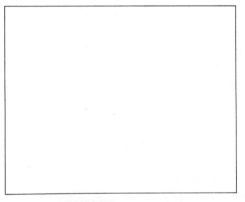

Edited by James W. Cox

with Patricia Parrent Cox

Abingdon
Nashville

THE TWENTIETH-CENTURY PULPIT, VOLUME II

Copyright © 1981 by Abingdon

Appendix copyright © 1978 by Abingdon

Scripture quotations noted RSV are from the Revised Standard Version
Common Bible, copyrighted © 1973 by the Division of Christian
Education of the National Council of the Churches of Christ in the U.S.A.,
and are used by permission.

Scripture quotations noted NEB are from the New English Bible. © the
Delegates of the Oxford University Press and the Syndics of the
Cambridge University Press 1961, 1970. Reprinted by permission.

MANUFACTURED BY THE PARTHENON PRESS AT
NASHVILLE, TENNESSEE, UNITED STATES OF AMERICA

Dedicated to

Lillian Mitchell Parrent
and
Overton Crockett Parrent,

who by their lives and service in the church have
magnified the message of the pulpit.

CONTENTS

FOREWORD

When I compiled Volume I of *The Twentieth Century Pulpit* a few years ago, I left out a number of sermons that I had wanted to include. Also, I obviously left out a number of worthy sermons I was not aware of at that time. This volume should rectify some of those omissions. It will not rectify all, for my tentative list for this volume had to be shortened even more drastically than before.

For the most part, these are sermons by a younger generation of preachers. This volume focuses more sharply on social and ethical issues, and on certain theological issues under current discussion, than did the earlier volume. Here, then, are examples of how preachers have struggled in the pulpit with various urgent matters. Readers will disagree at points with some of the preachers—with their beliefs and with their approaches. Yet they may find dialogue with these preachers stimulating in many ways. Pastors, for instance, may discover better methods for pulpit discussion of difficult themes; more important, they may have their understanding illuminated and their religious experience enriched; and most important, they may help their hearers to find fulfillment in the purposes of God.

Besides the persons whose sermons appear in this volume, many others have made helpful contributions. I am especially indebted to my wife, Patty, for her interest and advice and especially for her work with me on the biographical sketches. Others I wish to thank are: Samuel Baxter, Mrs. Nell Bellamy, Mrs. Sally Claybrooks, Kenneth Mitchell Cox, Wilbert B. Eichenberger, James M. Henry, Roy L. Honeycutt, Peter John, Charles H. Long,

Lee McGlone, R. Willard van Nostrand, Walter Shurden, William W. Smith, Wayne E. Oates, Dean Peerman, Evelyn and Frank Stagg, C. Penrose St. Amant, Marvin Tate, and Jeannie Willis. These latter persons have been helpful in various ways, though they are not responsible for contents of this book in general.

I have been pleased with the reception and wide use of *The Twentieth Century Pulpit* in the pastor's study and in the seminary classroom. This second volume is sent forth with the hope that it will be equally useful.

James W. Cox
The Southern Baptist Theological Seminary
Louisville, Kentucky

ELIZABETH ACHTEMEIER

Romanticism, Reality, and the Christmas Child

Old Testament Lesson: Isaiah 11:1-9
New Testament Lesson: Luke 2:22-35

*Behold, this child is set for the fall and rising of
many in Israel.*
                                        —Luke 2:34*b* RSV

We tend to romanticize Christmas. Heaven knows, we
don't mean to do so when we come into the first week or two
of the Advent season. You and I are, after all, very
hardheaded people. We know how to look after our own
interests. We know we have to stay on our toes in this
dog-eat-dog competitive society. We even know that
Christmas is just a momentary glow over the landscape of
an otherwise forbidding world, and that as soon as
January 2 rolls around and the angels have gone away into
heaven, and the carols are stilled, and the gifts put away,
we will all be back at it again—buying and selling and
scrambling after a buck, edging out academic competitors,
asserting ourselves, and maybe even stepping on the
fingers of the person below us on success' ladder.

   And yet, Christmas gets at us, doesn't it? The Scrooge in
us gives way to the innocence of Tiny Tim. The symbols
and songs and "Silent Night" work their magic glow, and
our hearts are warmed and our spirits lifted, and we find

This sermon was preached in Harvard Memorial Church on the Second
Sunday of Advent, December 1978. Used by permission of Elizabeth
Achtemeier.

ourselves beginning to hope that maybe, just maybe, things will work out all right after all.

It is at this point then, when our hopes are kindled, that the words of our text hit home: "The wolf shall dwell with the lamb, and the leopard shall lie down with the kid, and the calf and the lion and the fatling together, and a little child shall lead them. . . . The sucking child shall play over the hole of the asp, and the weaned child shall put his hand on the adder's den. They shall not hurt or destroy in all my holy mountain" (RSV). The picture calls forth all our romantic wistfulness—our hopes for a world quiet and at peace, where the serpent of our sin has been turned into harmlessness, where a soft lamb can curl up without fear before the fangs of the wolf, and the innocence and tenderness and sweetness of a little child dominate all relations. The Christ child, the newborn shoot from the stump of Jesse, the innocent babe lying in a manger—yes, that becomes the final symbol of our Christmas romanticism—the hope, the wonder, the love connected with the birth of a little child.

When the Scriptures seized on the figure of the child, however, and God incarnated his Son in a babe, they were not trying to be romantic and they were not indulging in our sweetness and light. For, you see, the figure of the child in the Bible is much more than a figure of salvation. Very often throughout the Old Testament, the child is also the figure of the Lord's coming judgment. There are all those children of the prophets, with those strange and ominous names given them by God. There is "Lo-ammi" in the Hebrew, the son of the prophet Hosea, whose name means "You are not my people." There is Hosea's other son, called by God, "Lo-rachamim," that is, "I will no longer have mercy upon you." And there is Isaiah's child, named to symbolize God's destruction of Israel; his name is translated, "The spoil speeds, the prey hastes," that is, Assyria will come upon you. A child, laughing and playing in the street, can be a prophetic symbol of destruction. When Isaiah wants to say that society will be dissolved, he foretells, "Babes will be your rulers" and "the youth will be insolent to the elder." And yes, when Jesus confronts his disciples' pride, he calls a child into their midst and warns them, "Unless you turn and become like children, you will never enter the kingdom of heaven." As in our Gospel lesson from Luke, a child, according to the biblical writers, can cause one to fall or rise. A babe can be an occasion for judgment or for salvation.

I wonder if we do not know that in our society these days, even more than we are willing to admit. W. C. Fields once remarked, with his marvelously cynical flair, "The person who hates dogs and children can't be all bad." And that used to be funny here in the United States because it wasn't true. But we are seeing some strange things happen to the image of children in our society. As a *Newsweek* column put it some time ago, American children are taking on the image of monsters. It is the child who is the bearer of evil in the movies *The Exorcist* and *Rosemary's Baby*. It is the child gone bad—with drugs and sex and vicious crimes—who is robbing our peace as citizens. "Americans do not like other people's children," wrote an Ohio State criminal justice expert recently, "especially the children of the poor. . . . The truth is that we are afraid of poor children, particulary those of other races. And like children of all classes, these children from time to time confirm our fears and our dislike of them by committing atrocious and frightening crimes" (John P. Conrad).

As a result, American society has begun to reject its offspring. Two years ago, Dear Abby made the mistake of asking her readers, "If you had it to do over again, would you have children?" She received ten thousand letters in response, and seven out of ten parents said no. Children were too much responsibility, was the reason, or they took too much time out of personal freedom. They disappointed their parents by the way they turned out, or they paid too little attention to those who raised them.

But that is not a judgment on the children as much as it is a judgment on the parents. And when we hear it all, we begin to get the feeling that something is terribly wrong. There is some sickness in this society we have made which is infecting our very offspring. Worse yet, there is some sickness in us which is making us warp and then hate our children. The child has become the symbol of judgment on our culture and on you and me. The child has become the instrument of our undoing.

So you see, the fact that Christmas has to do with a child, with a newborn babe in a manger, is not an event which should send us into unrealistic romanticism. The Christmas child, like all children, can be a judgment on us. And in fact, Jesus later tells us that he is the eternal child: "Whoever receives one such child," he says, "receives me" (RSV). Jesus comes to us first and eternally in the flesh and blood of a little child, and our attitude toward him can be an occasion of judgment, as well as of salvation. This child, the babe in the manger, the shoot from the stump of Jesse—this child, the Christmas child, is for the rise—and fall—of many.

Now what is it about the Christmas child which can make us stumble over him and turn him into an instrument of our own destruction? Surely the first mistake is to believe that we have no lasting responsibility toward him—like doting grandparents at the birth of a grandchild to admire and adore him on a ten-day Christmas visit, and then to return home to business as usual, with no more obligation toward him. For you see, this is a child of whom you and I are not going to be rid. This is in fact the eternal child—the one Herod's soldiers could not slaughter and the Roman Empire could not bury. This is God's child, the Lord's Messiah, the one on whom God has poured out his Spirit, and with his birth that Spirit now has invaded your lives and mine.

That's the fact that draws us irresistibly to Christmas in the first place, of course—the fact that our little realms are invaded by something beyond their borders, the fact that there floods into our darkness a light not dependent on our tarnished glories, the fact that some Spirit of wisdom and strength and understanding whispers in our hearts that perhaps there is a hope for our tattered lives after all.

But we shall be foolish indeed if we believe that Spirit abandons us on December 26, and that we need not answer thereafter to his persistent claim upon us. It is in truth Immanuel, God with us, in the birth of Jesus Christ, and we shall not be rid of him ever, ever again. "Whither shall I go from thy Spirit? Or whither shall I flee from thy presence? If I ascend to heaven, thou art there! If I make my bed in Sheol, thou art there!" (RSV). If we deny that fact, this Christmas child will be the occasion of our stumbling. This child, the Christmas child, is for the rise—and fall—of many.

The second mistake we can make is to think that we are immune from that judgment, and that the faith or goodness or importance or status we brought with us into this service this morning, is sufficient to guarantee the approval of our lives in the eyes of God. Somehow God does not see us in the same manner as we see ourselves. He sends a Son who is not swayed by the appearance of this world. "He shall not judge by what his eyes see, or decide by what his ears hear," reads our Old Testament text (RSV). Apparently our reputations and learning and self-confident appraisals of our own deserts are not important to the Almighty. Instead, he causes a little shoot to sprout forth from the rotten stump of history, and then he uses that branch as a yardstick to measure everything we have done.

We instinctively know that at Christmastime, too—that with the birth of Christ there has entered into our world a faithfulness which puts our vacillating trust to shame. There has come onto our scene one so pure that all our righteousness is shown to be smudged and dirty. There is a mercy now living in our midst which reveals most of our compassion to be self-seeking and calculating. And we are judged by Christ and shown by his light to be less than we ought to be. As Henrik Ibsen, at the age of sixty, wrote to an eighteen-year-old flirt, with whom he had become infatuated, "You and the Christmas season do not quite fit together."

This child, this Chistmas child, is for the rise—and fall—of many, and we shall make a terrible mistake if we think we are immune from the fall.

Good Christians, the Advent season is a season of repentance, the time when beyond all our wistfulness and romantic idealism and transitory feeings of goodwill, we take a sober, realistic look at ourselves and see that we are wanting. It is not enough any more to say with Thomas Hardy,

> If someone said on Christmas Eve,
>   "Come; see the oxen kneel,
> In the lonely barton by yonder coomb
>   Our childhood used to know,"
> I should go with him in the gloom,
>   Hoping it might be so. ("The Oxen")

It is not enough anymore simply to hope that Christmas might be so, merely to long for its spirit of peace on earth, goodwill toward men to endure throughout the year, piously to imagine that someday, somehow, our lives will have the innocency and brightness of its little child. Because, in truth, Christmas now is so, and measured against the hard reality of the branch from the root of Jesse, you and I are judged to be much, much less than we are supposed to be.

There *is* something wrong, something terribly wrong in our world, and in our personal lives. Our pride keeps getting in the way of our concern for other persons, for one thing. Our love for our comfort and the status quo undermines our zeal for justice, for another. Our wish not to be interrupted in our accustomed pursuits defeats our care for the outside world. And Advent is the season when we repent and confess that those things are so. Indeed, Advent is the time when we acknowledge that all our efforts at goodness have been futile, and that we are doomed and lost if we are left to our own devices. Our Old Testament lesson puts it in the figure of that lifeless stump: our history is barren and broken and fruitless, it is saying, and only God can make a new beginning. We are dead and clean cut off unless there is a shoot from the stump of Jesse.

Could it be, dear Christians, that rather than a season for romanticism, then, this Advent is precisely the time when we can, for once, be realistic? Could it be that we finally have the chance to be honest about ourselves—to pray, "Lord, my motives are terribly mixed, and my faith is constantly marred. Sometimes I am afraid and sometimes dreadfully lonely. I go on and on, but I often do not know where I am going. Lord, I have left undone those things which I ought to have done, and I have done those things which I ought not to have done. I have offended against thy holy laws, and now there is no health in me"?

Yes, Advent is the time when we can make such a confession, precisely because there is that shoot from the stump of Jesse, and precisely because if we will bow down before him, he will begin to lift us up.

This child, this Christmas child, does not want our destruction. He does not will that any one of us should fail before his judgment. He comes finally not to cause our fall, but to raise us up, to bring us forgiveness and healing and wholeness for our rebellious and sinful lives. As the Christmas carol has it,

> Light and life to all he brings,
> Risen with healing in his wings . . .
> Born to raise the sons of earth,
> Born to give them second birth.

But he comes as King, as final heir to the throne of David. That is what the Messiah is—God's chosen King. And unless we finish those words of that Christmas carol by the manner of our lives, unless we can truly sing,

> Hark! the herald angels sing,
> "Glory to the newborn king!"

unless we can, in repentance and humility turn our lives over to this Messiah, he cannot raise us up to newness and transformation of our way of living. It is only in humbling ourselves that we may be exalted. It is only in confessing our lack of wholeness and relying on Christ that we may be restored.

I was moved by the homily which our new pope, John Paul II, delivered in October, 1978, at his inauguration. "Do not be afraid to welcome Christ and to accept his authority," he told the nations. "Have no fear, open the doors. Fling them open to Christ and to His saving authority." And why should we be unafraid to do that? Because this child, the Christmas King, comes also as our Savior, set not only for the fall—but also for the rise—of many. If we acknowledge his rule, and rely on his Spirit at work in our lives for all our goodness, and look to him for the power to fulfill all his commandments, then we will, with the aged Simeon in our New Testament lesson, be able to say, "Mine eyes have seen thy salvation."

And so you see, it is finally not romantic nonsense to believe at this season of the year that we can be changed by Christ, to believe that he can pour out his sanctifying Spirit upon us, and cleanse our hearts and transform our ways to make them fit for Christmas. Not if we see that we come to that by the way of sober realism, by the way of deepest humility—by understanding our lives as they really are, by confessing that we need a King and Savior, and by trusting him to forgive and transform and guide and empower us.

Nor is it simply wistful daydreaming in Advent to look forward to that vision of Isaiah—that world of quiet and perfect peace filled with the knowledge of God, that picture of the lion and lamb, and our evil turned to harmlessness. That perennial human drama also takes on the shape of possibility, if we see that that world will also come because of hard reality—the hard reality of a criminal's cross and of a gaping, empty tomb.

This child, this Christmas child, knew our world of evil. Down the road of his life, past Bethlehem, beyond the angels and the glory and the shepherds, he met our wrong—every bit of it—on a hill called Golgotha: our strifes and hatred and our terrible distortions with which we warp our children; our injustice and apathy, and our awful pride with which we lay waste our world. He knew it all. He suffered it all. It nailed him to a cross. And he bore our evil and died our death and was buried with the world's destruction.

But he rose. He was raised from our death. He triumphed over all this world's wrong. And he promises us that if we trust his triumph, we may share his victory. This child, this Christmas King and Savior, *is set for the rise of many*. He promises us that his Kingdom comes, when every tongue will confess his rule, and yes, when they shall not hurt or destroy in all his holy realm, and the earth—his kingdom on earth—will be filled with the knowledge of God as the waters cover the sea.

Fantasy, friends? Wistful romanticism? Imagination gone wild at Christmastime? Oh no, it is all reality: as real as the flesh and blood of a newborn baby; as real as the evil in our lives and God's forgiveness of them; as real as a cross of death and the first rays of Easter morn. This child, this Christmas child, is set for your fall or rise. So repent. Trust him. Trust him to raise you up. And then have a merry Christmas.

Amen.

WALTER J. BURGHARDT, S.J.

Do We Deserve Peace?

When [Jesus] drew near and saw the city, he wept over it, saying: "Would that even today you knew the things that make for peace! But now they are hid from your eyes."

—Luke 19:41-42 RSV

I

Lord, we come before you a motley lot. We are wonderfully and dreadfully different. Some of us are violent in our convictions; others could not hurt a fly. Some of us have years behind us; the lives of others lie ahead. Some of us are knowledgeable, others quite ignorant. Some of us are happy people; others have forgotten how to laugh. Some of us have money; others must pinch and squeeze, beg and borrow. Most of us are white; only a few, I'm afraid, are black or yellow or brown. Some of us are settled, have it made; others are restless, trying to make it. Some of us have killed; others have seen death only on TV.

Some of us are awfully sure—about the war, about its morality or immorality, about ROTC and Dow Chemical, about American idealism or imperialism, about napalm and defoliation; others are confused, uncertain, torn this way and that, even anxious about our own uncertainty. Some of us think your Church is "out of it," a slave to the

This sermon was preached at a special Mass for Peace in St. Patrick's Cathedral, New York City, November 13, 1969. Reprinted from *Tell the Next Generation* by Walter J. Burghardt, S.J. © 1980 by Walter J. Burghardt, S.J. Used by permission of Paulist Press.

status quo, hidebound and a straddler; others feel she has gone too far too fast, runs after the latest fashion, is even heretical. Some of us have tasks that excite us; others go through motions from 9 to 5. Some of us have stored up hate in our hearts; others thrill with love. Some of us are neat and clean; others could not care less for middle-class hygiene. Some of us have come to terms with society; others have fled it or vowed to destroy it. Most of us are here because we still believe in you; some surely have come from curiosity, or custom, or even despair. A few of us may even be "effete snobs."[1]

Lord, we *are* a motley lot, aren't we?

II

Only one thing unites us at this moment, Lord: we all want peace. We are *all* convinced that war is hell. We *all* feel that there is something tragically wrong when the governments of the world spend 120 billion dollars a year to kill, to threaten, to deter, to keep peace. When a B-52 sets fire to fifty square miles so that nothing therein can live. When homes of the innocent are converted into incinerators. When the ratio of civilian-to-military casualties is three or five to one. When three million refugees water the roads and rice paddies with their tears. When human beings are tortured by other "human" beings.

We *all* weep for it, Lord—even those of us who feel that it cannot be otherwise, that it is not Christian, is not human, but must be. Even those who are soldiers or sailors or marines—who are trained to kill and to destroy—even they are nauseated at what they must do.

We all want life, Lord, and not death. We know the love and the anguish and the pain and the joy that goes into fashioning a single child. Many of us have shared with you the creation of life. We sense how precious each life is to you. And so we weep for each life that is snuffed out. We cannot rejoice when a headline proclaims that *only* two hundred Americans were killed this week; we cannot be glad when five thousand Viet Cong are flushed out and massacred. For these are not statistics, Lord; these are persons. And when even one shrieks to heaven with his flesh in flames—friend or enemy—we all weep, we are all ashamed, we all want peace.

III

We all want peace, Lord. The problem is, we are not agreed on how to get peace; we do not know "the things that make for peace." Oh yes, we have our convictions. There are those of us who "know" that the first step to peace is for us to get out, leave Southeast Asia. There are those who "know" that only all-out war will bring peace. And there are those silent millions somewhere in-between who don't want us to stay and don't see how we can go. And there are *all* of us who sense that, even if Southeast Asia is pacified, there is still the Middle East, there is Czechoslovakia, there are Libya and Bolivia, there is the whole vast continent of Africa.

We do not know, save superficially, "the things that make for peace." For some reason—perhaps for our sins—"they are hid from [our] eyes." If, as your prophet proclaimed, "peace is the fruit of righteousness" (Isa. 32:17), and if, as your Council taught, "peace is likewise the fruit of love,"[2] then war is the fruit of unrighteousness, of hate. But I dare not lay that unrighteousness, that hate, solely at the feet of the enemy, only in the heart of the politician—in Hanoi or Washington or Saigon. If I am as honest as I want my neighbor to be, I must look within, to see if the seeds of war are planted in my heart.

IV

And as we look, Lord, we must be distressed. Our love for human beings, we were told by your Son, our love would be the sacrament, the visible sign, that he is among us. This is how the world would recognize him. And the world does not see him, because the world does not see him in our love. Whole cities could live on the garbage from our dumps, on the clothes we wear once, on the luxuries we have made necessities. Black and white are threatened with bloody combat because we have been as color-conscious as our unbelieving neighbors. For so many of us, a court of law is more effective than the Sermon on the Mount. There is no evidence that we Catholics drink less, lust less, hate less than the men and women who never eat the flesh of your Christ or drink his blood. I am afraid we are what Paul called the pagans of his time: we are "faithless, ruthless, pitiless" (Rom. 1:31).

For all its own tyranny, what does Hanoi find in America, in us, to shake it, to make it marvel and cry, "Look how they love"? The seeds of war are within us, from the jealousy of Cain to the hate in my own heart, from the commerce that makes a jungle of the world to the ghettos we have structured for the Jew and the black, from the dishonesty of the little clerk to the tyranny of the big cleric.

A horrifying thought has just struck me, Lord: perhaps we do not *deserve* peace. Perhaps war is the logical fruit of our unrighteousness, of our personal hate, of our lack of love. It may be that what is happening in Southeast Asia began in our hearts, in my heart, not too long ago. No wonder your Son weeps over *our* city, saying: "Would that even today you knew the things that make for peace! But now they are hid from your eyes."

V

When we first came to you this evening, Lord, I think we came for a miracle, for your special intervention in the world, for a breakthrough that would change the heart of Hanoi, inspire our president, make the lamb and the lion lie down in Paris. I rather think now it is a different miracle we are asking. Just as you do not make wars, Lord, so neither do you end them. We make them, Lord, and so we have to end them. With your grace, of course; but unless *we* do it, it will not be done.

The miracle we ask, each of us, is a conversion. Change *us,* Lord. If we are unshakable on Vietnam, keep us from being unloving. If we are uncertain, let it not make us cowards. Take bitterness from us, even if we have cause to be bitter. Take hate from us, for we have never just cause for hatred. If we have bled, let the blood we shed be redemptive like your Son's. If we have grown fat—by our own honest industry or over the bodies of others—scourge us till we cry out. Each of us knows what it is within us that makes for war. Prick all our hearts with a sense of guilt; for we have sinned, Lord, all of us—we have sinned against peace.

VI

We are a motley lot, Lord; but do not let difference destroy love. Two days ago, in our Woodstock College community, two young guests threw from our dining room a large bowl of fruit, because it included some grapes, and the grapes might be from California. A young friend, also a guest, was asked by a Jesuit in the community if *he* had done this. He replied: "In the sense that the hands that did this were the hands of my brother, yes, I did it." He was pressed: "But aren't we your brothers too?" His answer, slow and serious: "I'm afraid I must say no."

Dear Lord, if this is the way we are, I weep, for we do not deserve peace. If we can love (as indeed we should) a hostile soldier on the other side of the Pacific, call him brother, can we not open our hearts to the human being next to us, despite our deep divisions?

That is why, Lord, in much hope and some fear, I am asking the men and women in front of me to take a first step toward peace. I am asking each to clasp the hand of the person next to him or her, the person on each side—whoever that person is, whatever he or she looks like—without even looking. I want them, by this act of faith and trust and love, to cry out to you that we do want peace, that we want to begin it here and now, that we see in each human being a brother or sister and the image of your Christ, that our hearts are open to them as never before, that we are ashamed and weep for our crimes against them. And I am asking them to sit like that, hands clasped, for one minute—all of us . . . for one minute . . . at peace.

NOTES

1. A reference to a caustic characterization of some adversaries by a high-ranking official in the Nixon administration around that time.
2. Vatican II, Constitution on the Church in the Modern World, no. 78.

JOHN R. CLAYPOOL

You Can't Have It All

Genesis 2:5-9, 15-17

During the academic year of 1968–1969, Sam Keen spent a
sabbatical leave in California studying the human
potential movement. He kept a journal of what he later
described as his "Jubilee Year," and on November 29,
1968, he entered the following words:

There are so many lives I want to live, so many styles I would like
to inhabit. In me sleeps Zorba's concern to allow no lonely woman
to remain comfortless. (Here am I, Lord, send me.) Camus'
passion to lessen the suffering of the innocent, Hemingway's
drive to live and write with lucidity, and the unheroic desire to
see each day end with tranquility and a shared cup of tea.

I am so many, yet I may be only one. I mourn for all the selves I
kill when I decide to be a single person. Decision is a cutting off, a
castration. I travel one path only by neglecting many. Actual
existence is tragic, but fantastic existence (which evades choice
and limitation) is pathetic. The human choice may be between
tragedy and pathos, Oedipus and Willy Loman. So I turn my back
on small villages I will never see, strange flesh I will never touch,
ills I will never cure, and I choose to be in the world as a husband
and a father, an explorer of ideas and styles of life. Yet perhaps
Zorba will not leave me altogether. I would not like to live
without dancing, without unknown roads to explore, without the
confidence that my actions were helpful to some.

As I have mulled over these highly personal words for
some time now, I have three distinct impressions. First of

Used by permission of John R. Claypool.

all, Keen is describing here the kind of world we all encounter day by day. Look in any direction you will, the truth remains: *we humans cannot have everything all at once.* Choice is built into the very essence of our existence. None of us can have it all. This is a rule that begins to apply to us the moment we are born into this world.

The writer of ancient Genesis recognized this fact. If you go back to the earliest of the two creation stories (Genesis 2), the very first thing said to the human creatures about life was this: "You can eat of all these trees, but not of that one. If you try to eat it all, you will surely die." In other words, from the very beginning there were more possibilities in life than the creatures had the capacity to actualize, more options out before humans than they had the energy or ability to fulfill. There is always more a person *could* do than a person *can* do, which means that choice is built right into the heart of our human constitution, and not to realize this fact is what Keen means by the term "pathetic." His suggestion that our human choice is always between tragedy and pathos is thus right on the point. Not to recognize that limits are a real part of the gift of life is the essence of pathos indeed.

I suppose we have all known folk who never learned this lesson, and the outcome of their lives is invariably disastrous. This was the case with the most gifted person in my high-school graduating class. He was stunningly brilliant intellectually, a wizard at both mathematics and science, and at the same time was a very talented musician and utterly articulate when it came to expressing himself. He was not terribly popular among his peers simply because he was so far beyond most of us in his capacities and development, and on graduation he won a scholarship to Columbia University in New York City. I honestly expected him to become nationally recognized someday because of his extraordinary promise, but before he reached his thirtieth birthday, he committed suicide. I never knew all the details, but it seems that he could never bring himself to say: "This one thing I do." Like Robert Frost, in his poem, he stood at a juncture where several roads branched out before him, and he tried to go down all of them at once, which simply does not work, even for genuises. He could not relinquish "the roads not taken," and that did make all the difference. This way of doing life really is pathetic, but one by no means escapes from pain by moving toward the other option and embracing the tragedy that is implicit in any decisive action. Our capacity to want is always greater than our capacity to have. There is something akin to cutting or killing when I decide to do this rather than that. I remember when this realization first broke over me with vividness. I was born in 1930, in the depth of the Great Depression, and one of the things our family never did was to go out to eat. Thus, when my sixth birthday came along, it really was something when I was told we were going out to Shakleford's Cafeteria on the corner of Fifth and Church to celebrate. It was the first time I can ever recall eating out. When we arrived, we stood in line for a long time in a narrow hall, and then suddenly there was a bend and before my eyes opened the grandest array of foods I had ever seen. Never before had I been in the presence of such abundance, and my first instinct was utterly predictable: *I wanted one of everything*—all the salads, all the pies, all the meats, everything. One look at my father made it clear that that was not possible; however, I think I knew that also on my own, young as I was. What was said to Adam and Eve in the Garden was applicable at that moment: "If you eat it all, you will surely die." This was my first inkling of the truth that too much even of a good thing becomes a bad thing, and so with some reluctance I opted for tragedy over pathos and picked out only one salad, one dessert, one meat, and so forth. However, the memory of what it was like to round that corner and see for the first time all the options a cafeteria affords lingers vividly in my mind, and is something of a symbol to me of the bittersweet thing it is to be our kind of creature in this kind of world.

What began to dawn on me then is a reality I have continued to encounter in one form or another up to this very moment. Just last week I ran into a friend of mine who has been very active in the feminist movement for the last decade, and she was reflecting to me how much things had changed in every way. "Years ago," she said, "my agony was having no choice—all those vocational doors that were arbitrarily shut to one because of gender. I thought then that if we could ever alter that condition, the kingdom of joy would come in. Of course, we have a long way to go, but there has been progress, and now, lo and behold, I face a new kind of agony—the agony of having to choose. It is a better agony, mind you, than the agony of having no choice, but it is an agony nonetheless." And I thought of Sam Keen's dictum that our human choice is always between tragedy and pathos. Painful as it is to have to relinquish the roads not taken, the one thing more painful is not to choose and wind up utterly fragmented. My first impression, then, was that Sam was being very realistic about this world in which we find ourselves.

My second thought, however, was that Sam was still having to struggle at an emotional level with what he was affirming at an intellectual level. He must have been in his late thirties when he wrote these words, and yet it seems to me that this vision of reality was "between his ears" but still had not gotten all the way down "into his insides," so to speak. But should this surprise us, really? Is not the process of internalizing truth a lifelong endeavor? Do we ever finish really the task of letting go our childhood fantasies of the way we wish things were and come home to actuality completely?

Anne Davis once pointed out to me that one way of looking at the temptation experiences of Jesus was to see them as a clash between the fantasies that grew out of his childhood and adolescence and the way he saw reality as an adult. What child among us has not dreamed that this was a world of magic rather than one of effort and struggle? The desire to snap one's fingers and have the stone before us turn to bread—who of us has not wished it were that easy? Or to be at one place and simply jump and be hundreds of miles away instantly—who of us has not so fantasized? Or the image of lying down before someone and having all things simply given to us without demand or effort on our part—this goes all the way back to our infant days when all was provided and nothing was expected. The point is that at thirty, Jesus was still having to struggle with how he would perceive reality and live in this world, and with no small struggle at each point he opted for actuality over against fantasy—the world as it is rather than the world of magic; but the struggle did not end there. One of the Gospels said the Tempter "departed for awhile," only to come again, which he did.

On into his ministry Jesus began to sense that what he had been sent to accomplish could not be done by words alone. He was going to have to make himself vulnerable to the worst in human nature; in other words, he was going to have to suffer, and when he began to share this with the disciples, Simon Peter challenged it and said, in effect: "There ought to be an easier way—some strategy of getting it done apart from suffering." I imagine even Simon was shocked by the vehemence of Jesus' response to this. He called Simon "Satan" and told him, "Get thee behind me," for Jesus sensed in those words the same temptation to fantasy that he had struggled with in the wilderness and managed to overcome.

And it lasted right up to the last night of his life. There in Gethsemane you see Jesus once again bringing the way he wished it was to the way it was, and literally sweating blood in the struggle to lay down the one and pick up the other. This is the struggle that goes on all the days of our lives, and thus I am not surprised to see Sam Keen having to struggle as an adult to come home emotionally to what he already knew intellectually. There is a sense in which Gethsemane is a paradigm for all of life—we never outgrow the struggle between fantasy and actuality—this bringing what we wish in the child part of our selves to the way it is as our adult part perceives it and choosing the one over the other. If there is a note of wistfulness and even sadness in Keen's decision to be "a husband and a father, an explorer of ideas and styles of life," that is not too surprising, really. None of us is finished yet; that is, reality is at some point in this pipeline between our heads and our hearts. None of us "has it all together yet," and we should not be dismayed that we still have to struggle to come to terms with reality.

But I have one other impression, and that is that things are not all bad in this existence of ours. To be sure, as we stand at a given crossroads, our choice is between pathos and tragedy—we cannot go down all the roads at once; but could we have it any other way and experience the special kind of joy God wanted for us? On more than one occasion I have raised my eyes to heaven and said: "Could you not have made it a little easier, God? Was there no way to create a world without such pain at the middle of all things human?" And when I have stayed with that question long enough to work it through, the answer comes back clearly: "No—this really is the best of all possible worlds if the experience of personal joy is the goal of all things." Stop and think about it for a moment: if there were not choices, how could any sort of personhood exist? If we could have everything, and never had to evaluate or set this over against that or go through the process of deciding, it would be simpler, but would it be better? Is not what I have described the experience of the animal kingdom? As best we know, animals are not burdened with the capacity of choice. There is no transcendence of experience for them—they simply want what they want when they want it, and they take it, and that is it—no pondering, no savoring first this possibility and then that, no acting, no looking back in satisfaction. And although such a process is unmistakably easier, I for one would have to say it is less, infinitely less, than what we humans experience. For all the agony that the power of choice brings into our lives, it is the secret of personhood—the source of our highest joy—and when you realize that this is why God created us in the first place, it begins to come clear: there was no other way. If we were to know his kind of joy—the sort of thing described in Genesis where God deliberately chooses to create and then acts decisively and then looks back and says: "It is good! It is good! It is very, very good!"—then we would realize that choice is absolutely essential. There is no other way to this kind of experience except through a process that exposes us to pathos and tragedy. To decide is to cut off, a form of castration; but once that is done, what lies down the road so painfully chosen is significant enough to make it all worth it. Once we stop weeping over the roads not taken and give ourselves with abandon to the things we can have and taste and see and feel and hear and smell, this is a joy of a real sort, akin to that which God as Person knows, and our true reason for being. It is true, we can't have it all, and to choose among the options is painful, even tragic. But do not forget, we can have some things. The trees that are available, the road that can be taken are all rich in potential beyond reckoning, and this is the note I would like to end on rather than the note I find in Sam's journal. There seems to be a mood of sad resignation in the decision to be "a husband and a father, an explorer of ideas and styles of life," rather than be a Zorba or a Camus or a Hemingway or whatever. But is such a fate so drab, really, if seized upon with relish and entered into with abandon? What I am saying is that the fact we cannot have everything should not blind us to the value of what we can have, and the exquisite privilege conferred upon us in being able to make choices at all. The very capacity of self-transcendence is a joy in itself. What is the burden of having to choose when compared to the state of having no choice at all? We have much to celebrate in the fact that there is abundance and we are not merely animals who are fated to do one thing and nothing else. We can choose and we do have alternatives, and I count that a joy which offsets the roads not taken and the many things we could do that we have neither the strength nor the opportunity to do.

Eugene O'Neill once wrote: "I can partly understand how God can forgive us humans, for we are so weak and foolish. But what I cannot understand is, how can he forgive himself for creating so painful a world?" I honestly do not think God is losing any sleep at this point. The joy he wanted us to experience could be on no other terms than our being persons of choice, and long ago he concluded, I think, that such a prospect was worth the risk. On this issue, I agree.

Is it not time, then, to stop whimpering about pathos and tragedy, and get on with the decision of which road we can travel and come to joy?

I think so—it is the point of this whole sermon. There is abundance and we can choose.

Let us begin!

WILLIAM SLOANE COFFIN, JR.

Iran

. . . and the government will be upon his shoulder . . .
—Isaiah 9:6

I know it's hardly great music, but there is one hymn I love to sing: "What a Friend We Have in Jesus." In Jesus we have a friend like unto no other. No other friend can fill our lives with such a presence. No other friend can so gladden the heart, liberate the mind and stretch the imagination. But it is also true that no other friend is more demanding. Old man Simeon foresaw this when he said of the child Jesus in his arms: "Behold, this child is set for the fall and rising of many in Israel, and for a sign that is spoken against . . . that thoughts out of many hearts may be revealed" (RSV).

It is often said that Christianity has been tried and found wanting. It would be more accurate to say that it has been tried and found difficult. It has been said that the weekly miracle of the churches is that we change the wine into water!

"And the government will be upon his shoulder." I've never been clear as to what that means but let's listen again to what Jesus had to say about love and hate: "You have heard that it was said, 'You shall love your neighbor and hate your enemy.' But I say to you, 'Love your enemies and pray for those who persecute you.'" (RSV). What does that say to us this morning if not, "You have heard it said, 'You shall love America and hate her enemies,' but I say to you, "Love the Ayatollah and pray for the students who persecute your fellow Americans in Teheran.'" Have you tried? It isn't easy, is it? Watching television, we get the impression that it is easy to be Iranian and Moslem these days. I am not sure, but I am sure that it is very difficult to be American and Christian.

Let's go back to the sermon on the mount.[1] "You have heard that it was said, 'An eye for an eye and a tooth for a tooth'" (RSV). Often that saying is misunderstood. Jesus is referring to a law which can be found in Exodus, Leviticus, and Deuteronomy, a law which underscores *one* eye for an eye, *one* tooth for a tooth. The law was necessary because the first method we humans devised to deal with our enemy was unlimited retaliation: "Kill my cat, and I'll kill your dog, your mule, and you too." The father/mother of this unlimited retaliation is of course the idea that might makes right—a thoroughly uncivilized idea, although one that still governs many actions of civilized nations today.

To the early Hebrews, however, it was clearer than it is to many of us that the end result of unlimited retaliation is mutual self-destruction. So a better way was sought, and there arose the notion of limited retaliation. In the twenty-first chapter of Exodus we read that in the event a person harmed another "then shalt thou give life for life, eye for eye, tooth for tooth, hand for hand, foot for foot, burning for burning, wound for wound, stripe for stripe" (KJV). Limited retaliation certainly is a step forward over unlimited retaliation. "Do unto others as they do unto you." "Get even, but no more." Limited retaliation is what most people have in mind when they speak of justice. It's the justification also most frequently used for capital punishment.

But Jesus then talks of a third stage, one that comes after unlimited and limited retaliation, one which we can call "limited love." "You have heard that it was said, 'You shall love your neighbor and hate your enemy.'" Actually in Leviticus 19:18 it is written: "You shall not take vengeance or bear any grudge against the [children] of your own people, but you shall love your neighbor as yourself" (RSV).

Again, a step forward. Limited love is better than limited retaliation. But when the neighbor has been limited to one of one's own people, then limited love has supported white supremacy, religious bigotry, the notion of "Herrenvolk," and "America for Americans," which, of course, never meant the Indians. Limited love is more self-serving than generous, as Jesus recognized when he said: "If you love those who love you, what reward have you? Do not even the tax collectors do the same? And if you salute only your brethren, what more are you doing than others? Do not even the Gentiles do the same?" (RSV).

Then comes the demand of which I spoke at the beginning: "You, therefore, must be perfect, as your heavenly Father is perfect." Without question, the translation presents a problem. The Greek word really means "to be perfected," or "completed," "finished"; it's the same that Jesus used on the cross when he said, "It is finished." So perhaps we could translate the sentence: "You, therefore, must be completely mature, even as your heavenly Father is mature." In other words, unlimited retaliation is babyish, limited retaliation is childish, limited love is adolescent. Only unlimited love that applies universally to all races and nations is evidence of maturity. It is God's desire that her children be as adult as she. In Advent, to prepare for the heavenly child we must become mature adults.

How all this applies to the present crisis in Iran is surely not as clear as the sky above us today. Lord knows our judgments are always subjective. No one has all the answers. If anyone did, it would simply mean he did not have all the questions! Nevertheless, we must strive to think as Christians; and to help us do so, let me add one more thought: "You have heard it said"—and then came a law; "but I say unto you"—and then came Jesus' understanding of the will of God. Jesus confronts the law with the will of God, insisting that the will of God is never something less and always something more than the law.

This is important because the United Nations' debate made clear last night that the great temptation today is not just to stay with limited love—think only of your own fellow Americans, your own fellow diplomats. There is also the temptation to think only of the law and its violations. There is no question about it: to invade an embassy and take hostages is to be in total violation of the law and to be against about every diplomatic tradition you can think of. So it is natural for Americans, and it is natural for diplomats, to say as so many do: "The hostages have to be freed. That is the first and only really important thing."

But suppose the government is to be upon his shoulder, not ours? Suppose we go from limited to unlimited love? The first thing we would have to do would be to put ourselves into Iranian shoes. If the will of God goes beyond the law, so do human relations. Human relations are finally not contractual. Human relations are finally just that—human. So the question we have to ask is not only, "What is legal?" but, "What is the human, moral, compassionate, imaginative thing to do for the good of all involved?"

Let's put ourselves in Iranian shoes. Clearly the Iranians think their moral, and even their legal, position is as strong if not stronger than ours. They think we are harboring a criminal, an Eichmann, only worse, because the Shah *gave* the orders, orders that imprisoned, tortured, and killed tens of thousands of Iranians. And they claim he absconded with millions of dollars. Some Iranians even think we are harboring him in the hope that we can put him back again on the throne. After all, it was not the choice of the Iranians but that of the CIA that put him there in 1953. So, if we try to move from limited to unlimited love, if we put ourselves in Iranian shoes, we can see that, morally speaking, we Americans appear to be living in a glass house, and people who live in glass houses shouldn't throw stones.

Two wrongs, however, don't make a right. They simply make two wrongs that need to be righted. Unfortunately, however, both the United States and Iran have sought to use the UN in an unprincipled way. Each side has sought to use the UN to right only the one wrong that has been done that side. But in a situation of unlimited love, both sides should try to rise above their present condition. Both sides, it would seem, should try to let the UN negotiate the release of the hostages and investigate the charges against the Shah.

There are two other things I think Christians should ponder. In the background of this problem is the broader one of tyrants deposed but not brought to trial. Since Nuremberg we have not tried any deposed tyrant. I am thinking of Idi Amin, Anastasio Somoza, Debayle, Pol Pot, Emperor Bocassa I. And I am thinking that if we have a legitimate international tribunal—something better than victors sitting in judgment, as at Nuremberg—then two things: (1) people wouldn't have to occupy other people's embassies in order to get their tyrants tried; and, (2) tyrants might be less tyrannical if they knew that one day they might be held not only morally but legally accountable for their misdeeds.

My final thought is this. I hope the Shah is tried, but it will not bother me one bit if he is tried *in absentia*. Cain killed Abel, but God, who doesn't believe in limited retaliation, does not kill Cain. God leaves Cain at the bar of history, a wonderful bar. I think that's where a ruler like the Shah should be left. I thought at the time how wonderful it would have been had the Israelis, after trying Eichmann, after putting the whole sad story before the whole world for the whole world to see—I thought it would have been wonderful had the Israelis turned to Eichmann and said: "OK, that's all, you can go. Like Cain you're marked; go wander the world." Because what is limited retaliation when it comes to an Eichmann, a Shah, an Idi Amin, a Pol Pot? And could there be justice without there being vengeance? And can justice without mercy ever be just?

I don't know. I do know that Jesus said, "Love your enemies and pray for those who persecute you," and I know that Advent is the time for unlimited love. This is the season in which we wait for him who will bear the government upon his shoulder.

I guess we have a lot to think about, and a lot to pray about too.

Bless, we beseech, O Lord, the Ayatollah with wisdom and compassion and President Carter with patience, for we'll never run out of time. Grant forbearance and kindness to the students guarding the hostages. May thine everlasting arms uphold the hostages and their loved ones. Grant us all, O God, a happy issue out of all our afflictions. Amen.

NOTE

1. The following owes a great deal to Clarence Jordan.

JAMES W. COX

God's Way into Our Lives

"He is not far from . . . us."
—Acts 17:27b RSV

God did not give us a caretaker's job when he put the gospel into our hands. To keep the church in smooth running order, to keep our traditions dusted and polished, or to keep a watchful eye on our family and special friends is not our main job. These things we must do. But he gave us a far bigger task. The world, with its triumphs and its despairs, its beauty and its ugliness, has moved next door to every one of us. Each day hurls new challenges at our faith.

This was true as long ago as the time of the apostle Paul. If Paul had limited his interests and concern to the Jews, his work would have been far simpler. No one had to tell him how Jews thought. He knew their Scriptures; he knew their traditions; he spoke their language. He was a Jew himself. But God flung him out into an intellectual wilderness where he had to forage in strange places for food for his Gentile audiences. Walking among the Greek philosophers, he found a scrap here and there which looked remarkably like the bread on which he had lived as a Jew. But the Greeks called him a "babbler"—a "seed-picker"—one who gathers up and gives out odd bits of the thoughts of others. Even so, he stuck out his neck and let them have their laughs. For his trouble he won a few people to Jesus Christ.

Today all sorts of ideas swirl about us like autumn leaves in a dust devil; the faces of people blur like the figures standing on a subway platform as we ride by; prayers lose themselves in the cries of the marketplace. And we find ourselves, the aspiring creators of a better world, trying to bring a semblance of order out of the chaos of the times.

I

Wouldn't it be much easier for us if we could be absolutely sure that God is at work in all mankind? Yet we are overwhelmed by the hurricane force of the demonic. It is often far easier to see Satan's hand than God's hand in the world, especially if we live where this hurricane force has struck again and again. Nations and factions will not quit fighting each other; the strong crush the weak; murder stalks the streets; charge and countercharge fly back and forth in the heat of political rivalry.

Nevertheless, God is at work. In a passage that catalogs some of the worst varieties of human evil, Paul wrote even of the wicked: "For what can be known about God is plain to them, because God has shown it to them. Ever since the creation of the world his invisible nature, namely, his eternal power and deity, has been clearly perceived in the things that have been made" (Rom. 1:19-20 RSV). God has revealed himself in his creation both by what he has made and by what he continues to do. No one can escape this revelation.

But it is not just the power of the sunset, the majesty of the universe, or the awesomeness of the unknown that moves men to recognize God. We have to do also with the work of his wrath. He makes himself known in anger and indignation. When idolatry has its innings and is out, when man reaps the harvest of his wrongdoing, when the universe impresses itself upon us as a moral universe, then we feel, "Surely God is at work!" And it makes sense. If God were not at work, how could we account for the prophet who rises out of the moral shambles of his times, declaring, "God commands all men to repent"?

It is true, God seeks us—but we are seeking after God,

too. We sometimes hotly deny it; we flee at the sound of his name; we try to hide from him among the things he has made, but in some way or other we want him. We pour out our ambitions and our passions upon a thousand altars—wealth, position, power, pleasure, and security in all their forms—and yet within our hearts we erect a secret altar to the unknown God. We run from God only to stumble into his arms.

Or we actively and consciously seek God, like Charles Haddon Spurgeon, the famous preacher of the past century, who as a teen-age lad wandered from church to church trying to find a merciful and forgiving God; or like the brilliant youth with the highest ethical code, who lingered after class with his philosophy professor, pressing him for reasons for believing in God.

As the Apostle put it, God has so made men "that they should seek God, in the hope that they might feel after him and find him. Yet he is not far from each one of us, for 'In him we live and move and have our being'" (Acts 17:27-28 RSV). This is the fact that looses upon us an avalanche of responsibility. Perhaps we ask, "What can we do?"

II

We can do several things.

For one thing, we can face the world and try, at least, to look every man in the eye. That in itself is a sort of victory, for we find it easy enough to steer clear of any situation that would make us uncomfortable or put us on the defensive with our faith. One encounter with an icily skeptical and critical person, and we are tempted to retreat to some cozy sanctuary, lick our wounds, and comfort ourselves with the promises of Christ to the persecuted.

Some interpreters think Paul did that: that he left Athens with a red face and downcast eyes, determined that from then on he would stick to his own ways of thinking and understanding and not dabble in the philosophical conceits of the Epicureans and Stoics. This might be so. Paul might have had excellent personal reasons for doing so; but this would not decide what you and I should do in a similar situation. Besides, I am not convinced that this is the last time Paul used his Areopagus tactics. Didn't he write to the Corinthian church, "For though I am free from all men, I have made myself a slave to all, that I might win the more. . . . I have become all things to all men, that I might by all means save some" (I Cor. 9:19, 22 RSV)? But we have to admit it is easier for most of us to avoid situations where we might be challenged and where there is a strong likelihood of failure.

If God is at work among all men, you and I don't have a one-sided selling job to do. Spiritual arm-twisting is neither permissible nor necessary. There is no room in Christian witnessing for the canned answer and the engineered decision. There is plenty of room for the kind of courage and honesty that makes a man as quick to say, "I don't know," as to say, "I know whom I have believed." The monolithic, impersonal "I'm right—you're wrong" approach to the unbeliever is deadly, even if we're right. Therefore, the way of friendly exchange and of positive witness is open to us provided we truly care about persons as persons and not as statistics.

Somehow we will have to find a point of contact with the people of our time. We have many things in common with our neighbors and with the people who work beside us: sports, the arts, government, books, and travel; home, children, food, taxes, and our aches and pains. But by point of contact I mean something deeper. When Paul walked among the Athenians, he was able, after the first heat of his anger at the idols had died down, to reconsider the religious beliefs of the Athenians for what they were worth. He cut through to the basic matter of what they believed, what they aspired to, and what they actually needed. He saw that the people before him had religious aspirations, just as he did, and openly acknowledged it. Then he went down the line with beliefs that he held in common with them. Because he started where they were, because he did not demand that they begin where he was, they listened.

43

We do not have to go far to discover how men live from day to day: what makes them swear, what keeps them awake at night, what makes the future look like a blind alley. We hear modern man saying such things as:

> "Life doesn't add up to anything."
> "I don't really mean anything to anybody—
> I'm just a statistic."
> "I wish I could be sure of something."
> "This world is run either by a devil or a lunatic."
> "I wish somebody could tell me what is right
> and what is wrong."[1]

Start talking with a man about the widespread feeling of the meaninglessness of existence, the depersonalization of our lives, the abyss of insecurity that undermines every certainty, the demonic in human affairs, and the ambiguities of ethical behavior, and right away you will have an audience. You will be talking about *him,* reading his secret sorrow, probing his pain and confusion, and in the process opening wellsprings of understanding. We ought not to be alarmed when we come up against skepticism and unbelief in the modern world: it only shows us our task in bold relief. Paul Tillich reminded us that the despair of our times reflected in much of modern art and drama poses the questions that it is the business of the Christian faith to answer. Any man's doubt is faith's opportunity.

III

It ought to be clear that a great duty is laid upon us in these days, a duty to attempt to lead men to a transforming experience of God, requiring us to prepare ourselves as Christian believers to do the job. We can see also that this is not a task to handle through our own wisdom and cunning. And we do not have to. Why?

Well, God has taken it upon himself to come to man, to break into history in such a way that we can take hold of him, to assume the burden of our ignorance and weakness and come in person to give us truth and power. Paul could go only so far with the Athenians on their own terms. There was a gap between the revelation of God in nature and the revelation of God in Jesus Christ. The world and the philosopher could tell some things about God, but not everything. God himself had to come and finish the story and show its meaning. And that is precisely what he did when Christ came. So men do not have to look until their eyes are red-rimmed, trying to see what the heavens say about God. Men do not have to fish around in their own minds to find the answer to the mystery of God. What men could never do, God himself has done. He has revealed what we could never discover. Christ the living Lord is in the world: he is God's response to man's groping hand that fingers the brooding mystery of the heavens.

Does this mean that when we present this Christ to the world with more expertise all our worries will be over, that men will be overwhelmed by the power of this revealed truth? Hardly. It did not happen when men stood face-to-face with Christ, when they saw his signs, when they heard his teaching, or when they heard the story of the resurrection. To some, Christ is a stumbling-block; to others, foolishness. When Paul finished his sermon in the Areopagus, where he had presented Christ in no uncertain terms, some mocked. So acceptance is not guaranteed. However, others wanted to hear more and a few believed. Therefore, "to those who are called, . . . Christ [is] the power of God and the wisdom of God" (I Cor. 1:24 RSV).

This revelation of God in Christ stands forever as God's way of getting at our hearts with his judgment and his mercy. And going right along with it, and absolutely necessary to it, is the work of the Holy Spirit. The Holy Spirit takes the event that happened two thousand years ago and makes it real and effective in lives today. When we bear our Christian witness, the God who raised Jesus Christ from the dead offers life to the dead spirits of those who hear us. Some of the best work of the Holy Spirit goes on after we have said good-bye and closed the door behind us, leaving a soul to his own thoughts. C. S. Lewis gave this account of his conversion: "You must picture me," he writes, "alone in that room in Magdalen, night after night, feeling, whenever my mind lifted even for a second from my work, the steady, unrelenting approach of Him whom I so earnestly desired not to meet."[2] This is why we dare believe that if we do not neglect our opportunities to give an intelligent, sincere testimony to the meaning of our faith, God can make every word we say weigh a ton.

The conclusion of this entire matter is this: the measurable results of our work may be disappointing, but we shall not fail if we are faithful to our task and accept God's standards of success. It was not an impressive number of disciples that followed Paul from the Areopagus, but there was one among them who, we are told, later became the respected bishop of Athens . . . , Dionysius the Areopagite. None of us can measure the far-reaching effectiveness of our work for Christ, for the gospel "is the power of God for salvation to every one who has faith, to the Jew first and also to the Greek" (Rom. 1:16 RSV).

NOTES

1. Compare H. H. Farmer, *The Servant of the Word* (Philadelphia: Fortress Press, 1942), pp. 89-109.
2. C. S. Lewis, *Surprised by Joy* (New York: Harcourt, Brace and Company, 1955), p. 228.

FRED B. CRADDOCK

Praying Through Clenched Teeth

"For I would have you know, brethren, that the gospel which was preached by me is not man's gospel. For I did not receive it from man, nor was I taught it, but it came through a revelation of Jesus Christ. For you have heard of my former life in Judaism, how I persecuted the church of God violently and tried to destroy it; and I advanced in Judaism beyond many of my own age among my people, so extremely zealous was I for the traditions of my fathers. But when he who had set me apart before I was born, and had called me through his grace, was pleased to reveal his Son to me, in order that I might preach him among the Gentiles, I did not confer with flesh and blood, nor did I go up to Jerusalem to those who were apostles before me, but I went away into Arabia; and again I returned to Damascus. Then after three years I went up to Jerusalem to visit Cephas, and remained with him fifteen days. But I saw none of the other apostles except James the Lord's brother. (In what I am writing to you, before God, I do not lie!) Then I went into the regions of Syria and Cilicia. And I was still not known by sight to the churches of Christ in Judea; they only heard it said, 'He who once persecuted us is now preaching the faith he once tried to destroy.' And they glorified God because of me."

—Galatians 1:11-24

Used by permission of Fred B. Craddock.

I am going to say a word, and the moment I say the word I want you to see a face, to recall a face and a name, someone who comes to your mind when I say the word. Are you ready? The word is "bitter." Bitter. Do you see a face? I see a face. I see the face of a farmer in western Oklahoma, riding a mortgaged tractor, burning gasoline purchased on credit, moving across rented land, rearranging the dust. Bitter.

Do you see a face? I see the face of a woman forty-seven years old. She sits out on a hillside, drawn and confused under a green canopy furnished by the mortuary. She is banked on all sides by flowers sprinkled with cards: "You have our condolences." Bitter.

Do you see a face? I see the face of a man who runs a small grocery store. His father ran the store in that neighborhood for twenty years, and he is now in his twelfth year there. The grocery doesn't make much profit, but it keeps the family together. It's a business. There are no customers in the store now, and the grocer stands in the doorway with his apron rolled up around his waist, looking across the street where workmen are completing a supermarket. Bitter.

I see the face of a young couple. They seem to be about nineteen. They are standing in the airport terminal, holding hands so tight their knuckles are white. She's pregnant; he's dressed in military green. They are not talking, just standing and looking at each other. The loudspeaker comes on: "Flight 392 now loading at Gate 22, yellow concourse, all aboard for San Francisco." He slowly moves toward the gate; she stands there alone. Bitter.

Do you see a face? A young minister in a small town, in a cracker box of a house they call a parsonage. He lives there with his wife and small child. It's Saturday morning. There is a knock at the door. He answers, and there standing before him on the porch is the chairman of his church board, who is also the president of the local bank, and also the owner of most of the land round about. The man has in his hands a small television. It is an old television, small screen, black and white. It's badly scarred and one of the knobs is off. He says: "My wife and I got one of those new twenty-five-inch color sets, but they didn't want to take this one on a trade, so I just said to myself, 'Well, we'll just give it to the minister. That's probably the reason our ministers don't stay any longer than they do, we don't do enough nice things for them.'" The young minister looks up, tries to smile and say thanks. But I want you to see his face. Bitter.

Will you look at one other face? His name is Saul, Saul of Tarsus. We call him Paul. He was young and intelligent, committed to the traditions of his fathers, strong and zealous for his nation and for his religion, outstripping, he says, all of his classmates in his zeal for his people. While he pursues his own convictions, there develops within the bosom of Judaism a new group called Nazarenes, followers of Jesus. They seemed at first to pose no threat; after all, Judaism had long been broadly liberal and had tolerated within her house of faith a number of groups such as Pharisees and Sadducees and Essenes and Zealots, so why not Nazarenes? As long as they continue in the temple and in the synagogue, there's no problem.

But before long, among these new Christians a different sound is heard. Some of the young radicals are beginning to say that Christianity is not just for the Jews but for anyone who believes in Jesus Christ. Such was the preaching of Stephen and Philip and others: it doesn't really matter if your background is Jewish as long as you trust in God and believe in Jesus Christ. This startling word strikes the ear of young Saul. "What do they mean, it doesn't matter? It does matter! It is the most important matter. No young preacher can stand up and say that thousands of years of mistreatment and exile and burden, of trying to be true to God, of struggling to be his people and keep the candle of faith burning in a dark and pagan world mean nothing. What does he mean, it doesn't matter to have your gabardine spat upon, and to be made fun of because you are different? Of course, it matters!"

Imagine yourself the only child of your parents, but when you are seventeen years old, they adopt a seventeen-year-old brother for you. When you are both eighteen, your father says at breakfast one morning: "I have just had the lawyer draw up the papers. I am leaving the family business to our *two* sons." How do you feel? "This other fellow just got here. He's not really a true son. Where was he when I was mowing the lawn, cleaning the room, trying to pass the ninth grade, and being refused the family car on Friday nights? And now that I'm eighteen, I suddenly have this brother out of nowhere, and he is to share equally?" How would you feel? Would you be saying, "Isn't my father generous?" Not likely.

Then imagine how the young Saul feels. Generations and generations and generations of being the people of God, and now someone in the name of Jesus of Nazareth gets this strange opinion that it doesn't matter anymore, that Jews and Gentiles are alike. You must sense how Saul feels. All your family and national traditions, all that you have ever known and believed, now erased completely from the board? Every moment in school, every belief held dear, every job toward which your life is pointed, now meaningless? Everything that grandfather and father and now you believed, gone? Of course, he resolves to stop it. The dark cloud of his brooding bitterness forms a tornado funnel over that small church, and he strikes it, seeking to end it. In the name of his fathers, in the name of his country, in the name of God, yes.

Now, why does he do this? Why is he so bitter at this announcement of the universal embrace of all people in the name of God? Do you know what I believe? I believe he is bitter and disturbed because he is at war with himself over this very matter. And anyone at war with himself will make casualties even out of friends and loved ones. He is himself uncertain, and it is the uncertain person who becomes a persecutor, until like a wounded animal he lies in the sand near Damascus, waiting for the uplifted stroke of a God whom he thinks he serves.

But Paul knows his is a God who loves all creation. He knows; surely he knows. Saul has read his Bible. He has read that marvelous book of Ruth, in which the ancestress

of David is shamelessly presented as a Moabite woman.
Certainly, God loves other peoples. He has read the book of
Jonah and the expressed love of God for people that Jonah
himself does not love. Paul has read the book of Isaiah and
the marvelous vision of the house of God into which all
nations flow. It is in his Bible. Then what's his problem?
His problem is the same problem you and I have had
sometimes. It's one thing to know something; it's another
thing to *know* it. He knows it and he does not know it, and
the battle that is fought between knowing and really
knowing is fierce. It is sometimes called the struggle from
head to heart. I know that the longest trip we ever make is
the trip from head to heart, from knowing to knowing, and
until that trip is complete, we are in great pain. We might
even lash out at others.

Do you know anyone bitter like this; bitter that what
they are fighting is what they know is right? Trapped in
that impossible battle of trying to stop the inevitable
triumph of the truth? Do you know anyone lashing out in
criticism and hatred and violence against a person or
against a group that represents the humane and caring
and Christian way? If you do, how do you respond?
Hopefully you do not react to bitterness with bitterness.
We certainly have learned that such is a futile and
fruitless endeavor, just as I hope we have learned we do not
fight prejudice with prejudice. A few years ago, many of us
found ourselves more prejudiced against prejudiced people
than the prejudiced people were prejudiced. Then how do
we respond?

Let me tell you a story. A family is out for a drive on a
Sunday afternoon. It is a pleasant afternoon, and they
relax at a leisurely pace down the highway. Suddenly the
two children begin to beat their father in the back: "Daddy,
Daddy, stop the car! Stop the car! There's a kitten back
there on the side of the road!" The father says, "So there's a
kitten on the side of the road. We're having a drive." "But
Daddy, you must stop and pick it up." "I don't have to stop
and pick it up." "But Daddy, if you don't, it will die." "Well,
then it will have to die. We don't have room for another

51

animal. We have a zoo already at the house. No more animals." "But Daddy, are you going to just let it die?" "Be quiet, children; we're trying to have a pleasant drive." "We never thought our Daddy would be so mean and cruel as to let a kitten die." Finally the mother turns to her husband and says, "Dear, you'll have to stop." He turns the car around, returns to the spot and pulls off to the side of the road. "You kids stay in the car. I'll see about it." He goes out to pick up the little kitten. The poor creature is just skin and bones, sore-eyed, and full of fleas; but when he reaches down to pick it up, with its last bit of energy the kitten bristles, baring tooth and claw. Sssst! He picks up the kitten by the loose skin at the neck, brings it over to the car and says, "Don't touch it; it's probably got leprosy." Back home they go. When they get to the house the children give the kitten several baths, about a gallon of warm milk, and intercede: "Can we let it stay in the house just tonight? Tomorrow we'll fix a place in the garage." The father says, "Sure, take my bedroom; the whole house is already a zoo." They fix a comfortable bed, fit for a pharaoh. Several weeks pass. Then one day the father walks in, feels something rub against his leg, looks down, and there is a cat. He reaches down toward the cat, carefully checking to see that no one is watching. When the cat sees his hand, it does not bare its claws and hiss; instead it arches its back to receive a caress. Is that the same cat? Is that the same cat? No. It's not the same as that frightened, hurt, hissing kitten on the side of the road. Of course not. And you know as well as I what makes the difference.

Not too long ago God reached out his hand to bless me and my family. When he did, I looked at his hand; it was covered with scratches. Such is the hand of love, extended to those who are bitter.

MILTON CRUM, JR.

The Christmas Story and Our Stories

The Christmas story equals a faith story by which we
make sense of our life stories.
We use faith stories to make sense of life stories.
For example
     in your life story
   something good happens
 and you make sense with a faith story, like,
"Lady Luck was on my side."
Our life stories tell what happens;
 our faith stories make sense of what happens.
I want to share with you the Christmas faith story as I read
it and how it makes sense of my life story.

I

If I were writing the Christmas faith story the way I
       would like it
   I would have Jesus born in a comfortable home
 or hospital
with the best medical care.
He would grow up in a stable neighborhood
  surrounded by friends
 and family.
He would live in a nation
  marked by peace
 and prosperity.
He would enjoy a long and happy life.

II

But, the biblical faith story is not that way at all.
The biblical faith story is a most unlikely story:
>   Mary and Joseph
>   newlyweds with troubles of their own
> had to make a
>   long
>   hard
>   costly
>   trip
because a foreign emperor wanted to squeeze more tax
money from their tiny land.
Feel their helplessness
>   under the power
>   of a cruel
> autocratic government.
Feel their frantic efforts
>   to find a room to sleep
>   to have a baby.
Feel their loneliness
>   and fear
>   in the crush of strangers.

They made it through the birth, but then found out Herod
was trying to kill the baby.
Feel the terror
>   of someone
>   trying to kill *your* baby.
They did the only thing they could;
>   they fled the country;
>   escaped to Egypt.
Feel the confusion
>   of being a refugee
>   in a strange land.
There was not a home for them anywhere.

Back in Judea,
>   feel with the parents whose babies had been
>   killed:

Why my baby?
What has an innocent baby done to deserve this?
What have I done to deserve this?
Feel the guilt Mary and Joseph must have felt:
Because of their baby
thousands of babies were killed.
If they hadn't fled to save their baby
all the other babies would be alive.

They survived the escape to Egypt;
and when they heard Herod was dead
they planned to go back home.
But, they learned that another wicked king, Archelaus,
had replaced Herod.
So they could not go home;
they had to go to Nazareth instead.
Feel the frightening insecurity of the Holy Family.
Feel the anxiety of the ominous.

To make the biblical Christmas faith story even more
unlikely
it is told as God's working his purpose out.
What was happening in the Christmas story
God had decreed in the Old Testament.

God had decreed
that the Savior was to be born in Bethlehem
so Caesar was merely an instrument of God
in ordering Joseph and Mary to go to Bethlehem.

God had decreed
there would be weeping in Judea
and that his Son would be called out of Egypt
so Herod was merely an instrument of God.

God had decreed
that Jesus would be a Nazarene
so Archelaus in today's gospel was merely an
instrument of God.

So, the biblical Christmas story is an unlikely story in two ways:

    a. It is not the happy story that a Christmas story ought to be.

    b. God is depicted as doing unlikely things.

III

Yet, this is the Christmas faith story which the Bible gives us to make sense of our lives.

And, I must admit that the Christmas faith story the Bible tells

          does better at making sense of life than the
                Christmas story
   the nice one
I would like to write.
For the Merry Christmas story of
     "once upon a time . . .
    they lived happily ever after"
  is nobody's story, is it?
So the nice Christmas story I would like to write is really the unlikely story isn't it?
The biblical Christmas story is much more likely to happen in real life,
so it does much better at making sense of life.

Sometimes, we get stepped on by a powerful Caesar.
Sometimes, we get pushed around by powerful Herods.
So many things happen to us that we cannot control:
        from fifteen-cent stamps to income taxes
      from the cost of groceries to interest rates
    from local vandalism to international war
   from missing a promotion to losing a job
  from a headache to a heart attack,
things happen to us which we can't control and we begin to feel helpless.

And, we see undeserved suffering
   like innocent children killed by Herod
   and we begin to feel that the end of life is tragic.

And, like the Holy Family,
      we try to escape—
      escape into whatever "Egypt" we can,
   because we begin to feel that life is too much to cope
         with.
On the level of actuality, the biblical Christmas story says
         yes
      these are the kinds of things that happen to people,
   to us.
The biblical story is the actual human story.
But, on the level of faith, the biblical story says no:
      No, we are not helpless.
   No, the end of life is not tragic.
   No, life is not too much to cope with.
The biblical Christmas story tells us:
      No, we are not helpless.
   Our God, in Jesus Christ
   lived through all these things.
He is with us; he shares everything in life with us.
He walks with us; he holds our hands.
But, not only is he with us:
      He is God Almighty
   ruler over all Caesars and Herods.
He is God Almighty over all suffering and death.
The final outcome of everything is in God's hands.
Therefore
      No
   we are not helpless.
By the power of God before whom we kneel in trust at his
table,
      we have confidence
      and strength
   to face life standing up.
No, life is not finally tragic.
Yes, there are tragedies in our life stories

but the biblical story
points beyond the tragedies
to new life in Christ
on earth
or in heaven.

No, life is not too much to cope with.
We cannot cope with everything;
But we can cope with the portion God assigns us.
The Bible promises us that God will not give us more to
cope with than we can handle.
He may give us difficult and painful assignments
but not impossible ones.

ELAM DAVIES

All Things New?

*And I saw a new heaven and a new earth: for the
first heaven and the first earth were passed away;
and there was no more sea. . . . And he that sat
upon the throne said, Behold I make all things
new.*

—Revelation 21:1, 5 KJV

Let's talk about the end—or should we say, beginning?
What does a Christian believe about life after death? I
want you to note the point of the question. We are not
asking *whether* we believe in another world, or our
existence in it. For the Christian, this has been answered
once and for all. Without a blush the writers of the New
Testament say, "Because he lives, we shall live also." That
settles it for them and for us. We do not argue about an
inherent immortality of the soul; we talk about the power
of the resurrection. "For half a century," said Victor Hugo,
"I have been writing my thoughts in prose and verse,
history, philosophy, drama, romance, tradition, satire,
ode, song. But I feel that I have not said a thousandth part
of what is in me. When I go down to the grave, I shall have
finished my day's work. . . . Another day will begin next
morning!" What kind of a day? What will it be like there?

The moment we seriously begin to address ourselves to
this question we realize how little we know, how little
indeed we can know. The veil of sense hangs heavy
between, not because God would keep us in ignorance for

From *This Side of Eden* by Dr. Elam Davies. Used by permission of the
Fleming H. Revell Company.

ignorance' sake, or in order to remind us of our creaturely status, but because to know a great deal more would unfit us for what Keats calls "this vale of Soul-making." This much is fairly evident, and it can be shown by a number of things.

Have you ever sensed the restraint found in any New Testament descriptive account of the life to come? Excitement may be raised to fever pitch when the Apostle Paul in one of his letters tells us that he knew a man once who was raised to the third heaven, Paradise; and then our hopes are quickly dashed on the rock of restraint when we continue to read, ". . . and he heard things that cannot be told, which man may not utter" (II Cor. 12:2-4 RSV). Isn't it frustrating? John Baillie was right when he said, "Many a celestial geography has been committed to paper, many a chart has been traced of the New Jerusalem, many a classified directory has been compiled of its various denizens," but all to no avail. In vain we seek to force the restraint, and we make a laughingstock of ourselves when we try to turn the poetry of Revelation into cold unimaginative prose.

That much fuller knowledge of the world to come would unfit us for the one we are in, may be gathered from the authentic mood in which the maturest of Christians have faced eternity. Their outlook has been characterized by a genuine sense of adventure. Listen to the old disciple in Ephesus, the last survivor of the Twelve, a man well in his nineties: "Beloved, we are God's children now; it does not yet appear what we shall be, but we know that when he appears we shall be like him, for we shall see him as he is" (I John 3:2 RSV). John's days were over. He had no business feeling so excited, by any reasonable standard of calculation; but somehow he had learned the secret of perpetual youth: the future is resplendent with new possibilities.

A great preacher used to tell the story about an old Indian Army officer who was a clever public speaker. He would delight his audiences with stirring tales, vividly describing his skirmishes, sieges, and hairbreadth escapes. As he worked upon the imagination and feelings of his listeners, he would suddenly stop and, after a dramatic pause, would continue, "I expect to see something much more wonderful than all that I have seen already." He was well over seventy years of age, and it was obvious that his audience received his charged announcement with skepticism. But in seconds it was gone when he continued, "I mean, in the first five minutes after death!" No doubt we can catch the sense of adventure; we may even appreciate the mood of excitement—but can we enter into it?

Perhaps what disturbs us is not that we know so little, but that deep down in our hearts we may be a little crestfallen about what we know. Take, for example, the glorious affirmation in the Book of Revelation, "Behold, I make all things new" (21:5). Does the idea tug at your heart a little bit? Newness has a great appeal, but as you go on in life, familiar things, some old things, take on precious meaning. Could it be that the life hereafter is so different that we would be utterly lost in it?

Dr. W. A. L. Elmslie, onetime principal of Westminster Theological College in Cambridge, England, a man of fine humor, a brilliant Old Testament scholar, and a superb golf player, in one of five broadcasts which had wide popularity during the last war, described how the Jewish view of things to come was translated into the Christian and changed. One good Jewish achievement was the attempt to portray the joy of heaven. "Poetic use was made of a supremely joyous occasion in Jewish life, namely, the reunion of friends and brethren at a great festival of worship at Jerusalem. So men pictured a heavenly counterpart to Jerusalem, its streets of gold, its gates of pearl, thronged with harps, the chanting of psalms. Life brings us differing memories of happy times on earth. Thousands of lads and lassies in Manchester, Leeds, and Sheffield cherish thoughts of golden hatless days on the moors. I sometimes hunger for an ideal golf course with a heavenly day for the game, and then work God thinks I should do for him. I can't play the harp, and though I like to study the Hebrew Psalms, I'm sure the singing of them is best left [looking around at the B.B.C. singers] to some who are present with me here tonight!"

We get the point quickly, don't we? If each one of us could fashion his own heaven, it would be hell for many others! But "all things new"! New heaven, new earth, no more night, no more sun, no more sea! There are treasures of darkness, there are transforming wonders of sunrise and sunset, and there is the azure beauty of the horizon-lapping ocean. What do you imagine a sentence like "And there was no more sea" means to one practically cradled in the sound of the crashing ocean wave?

How prosaic can we get? What did the seer banished to Patmos dread most? It is hard to say. His isolation accentuated the hurting power of the physical forces. The relentless heat of the sun by day, the lonely horrifying hours of the dark by night, and always the mortal enemy—the sea, the symbol of his final separation from those he loved. Whatever else the "hereafter" will mean for the Christian, there will be no more separation, no more heartbreaking loneliness, no more fruitless longing. How great a disservice we do this man by translating into literalities the answers God gave to the deepest needs of his soul.

But can "hereafter" be described only by negation, by saying what it is not? Is the best we can do to delineate what we shall *not* experience or feel or see? No! There are positive convictions which the writers of the New Testament and the saints through the ages long to share with us. I will begin with the most important.

The life to come is a life of vision. "We shall see him," the writers of the New Testament say. Down through the centuries the church has spoken with awe about the "beatific vision." This is not the gaze of the curious, the discovery of the excited, the boast of the successful, but the "vision" which comes slowly and wondrously to those who are humble of heart. It is the eternal exploration of the majestic Being of God, "whom eye hath not seen," through an understanding of, and growth in, the likeness of Jesus Christ. Bernard of Cluny's hymn, "Hic Breve Vivitur, Hic

Breve Plangitur," translated by John Mason Neale, contains these beautiful stanzas:

> The morning shall awaken,
> The shadows shall decay,
> And each true-hearted servant
> Shall shine as doth the day.
>
> Yes! God, our King and Portion,
> In fulness of His grace,
> We then shall see for ever
> And worship face to face.

But more. The life to come is *a life of service:* ". . . his servants shall serve him" (Rev. 22:3 KJV). We begin to see after a while that the meaning of "all things new" is a reference to that which man at his best seeks and often misses. There are old, old values which become more and more precious in the world to come, and among them the desire for service, the means for service, the power for service, and the scope for it. Heaven is not a holiday; it is not retirement, but service with joy, free from the limitations of this flesh, so fickle, so weak, so unsure of itself.

Some years ago I was startled by one of my parishioners as he left church on a Sunday morning. "I have a message for you," he said, and when I asked, "From whom?" he proceeded to name a revered colleague who had died a number of years before. One of the unwritten rules in a clergyman's life should be, "Never be surprised by what you hear after a Sunday morning's sermon," and that day I tried to hide the lack of composure and the degree of skepticism I felt within. The circumstances cannot be told here, but they were, to say the least, impressively uncanny. There was more than one message—one in particular was a "word" from a devoted Christian man who after years of service as a company director had offered his services to the community after his "retirement." I am not commenting now on the validity or otherwise of psychical research. What interested me then was not whether such messages were possible, but what kind of "message" came. "I thought I had come to heaven for a rest after a busy life. Was I mistaken! I have been busier here on more important work than I had ever dreamed possible on earth!" If you had known my friend, you would have caught the underlying humor. If you know your New Testament, you know how instinctively right is the conviction.

Only those who have lived in a Welsh village, who have heard the hillsides ring with the melodious voices of miners singing unrehearsed and unaccompanied—in perfect harmony—can appreciate the moving splendor of one of the favorite hymns sung at their funeral services, "O Fryniau Caersalem Ceir Gweled":

> From heavenly Jerusalem's towers
> The path through the desert they trace,
> And every affliction they suffered
> Redounds to the glory of grace. . . .
>
> And we, from the wilds of the desert,
> Shall flee to the land of the blest;
> Life's tears shall be changed to rejoicing,
> Its labors and toils into rest.

One almost feels a traitor to one's tradition to question the validity of the last line. But if the truth be told, it must be questioned. I like the somber singing in the minor key, somber but triumphant too, but I don't accept the underlying sentiment about the "final rest." Of course, such "rest" must be defined. If it means rest from fruitless and frustrating toil, then it is right. But if it means rest in the absolute sense, a cessation from active and fruitful service, then, however traumatic, I must choose to substitute them by the lines written by an *Englishman!*

> Free from the fret of mortal years,
> And knowing now Thy perfect will,
> With quickened sense and heightened joy
> They serve Thee still.

Most importantly, *the life hereafter is a life lived in love*. John Greenleaf Whittier has a beautiful poem, "The Brother of Mercy," in which he describes how an old monk who had spent his days in self-denying work for others came at last to the "valley of the shadow." Rather abruptly his confessor told him that his work was done:

> Thou shalt sit down and have endless prayers,
> Wear a golden crown for ever in Heaven.

But the old monk protested. He was a stupid old man, dull at prayers. He couldn't keep awake, but he loved his fellow man and could be good to the worst of them. He could not bear to sit among the "lazy saints" and turn a deaf ear to the sore complaints of the needy. He would have no idle heaven. He wanted to work for others. In anger, the confessor turned away from him, but that night he heard the voice of His Lord:

> Tender and most compassionate one. Never fear,
> For Heaven is love, as God himself is love;
> Thy work below shall be thy work above.

To many of us, that may well be a depressing thought until we pause to reflect that Whittier was not speaking of the things we do, but of the spirit in which they can be done, the love which grows ever and through eternity. All things will become new through a very old power, a power as old as divinity itself, the power which we as yet have never seen fully at work—except on a cross.

D. W. CLEVERLEY FORD

The Trinity

*The rain came down, the floods rose, the wind
blew, and beat upon that house; but it did not fall,
because its foundations were on rock.*
                              —Matthew 7:25 NEB

I would like us all to imagine for a moment that each one of
us is given a spade, told to go outside the church, and to
start digging about one yard away from the walls of this
building. When our imaginations have survived the shock
of the backache that would be involved, we might inquire
what we expected to find. Worms, of course, perhaps
human bones. I've seen such turned up before now in
ground close to a church, but what is it that we would be
bound to find? The foundations, the basis on which this
building stands. And these foundations might surprise us.
When York Minster was being restored, the foundations
under the great east window were found to be alarmingly
inadequate. When All Souls, Langham Place in London,
was recently being excavated in order to construct a hall
underneath the nave, the whole church was found to stand
on inverted arches just as if a church has been placed on its
back with its nave columns sticking up into the air like an
animal's legs. Yes, foundations are surprising.

But now let us venture on another expedition. Not this
time into the churchyard, each groaning with an un-
wieldly spade, but down underneath all the paraphernalia
of church life as we know it—bishops, clergy, choristers,
churchwardens, rural deans, synods, Mother's Union,

Used by permission of D. W. Cleverley Ford

boards of finance, vestments, candles, altars, the Prayer Book and the little books we have been struggling with recently, the missionary societies, the industrial chaplaincies, the creeds, the catechism—indeed, everything you can think of connected with church. Go down, right down underneath, what do you find? On what is everything built? It is the Trinity—God the Father, God the Son, God the Holy Spirit. Dig right down and you will find this foundation of our whole Christian way of life. God the Father, God the Son, God the Holy Spirit, the Trinity.

And now someone in the congregation is beginning to groan. Here comes the heavy stuff, you say, just as if we *could* be expected to listen to theology on a lovely summer evening. But look, the world isn't uniformly beautiful. Everything in the garden isn't lovely. Sometimes people ask, how do you explain if this is God's world, the tsetse fly, the hook worm, bacteria, and rabies? And in London hospitals I've seen children born deformed, crooked, and diseased from birth. Not long ago I visited two of London's major prisons. There is nothing beautiful about Wandsworth or Wormwood Scrubs. Let me say this with all the force I can command, whatever you may say about the first line of the Apostles' Creed, expressing belief in the first person of the Trinity, it just isn't trite, sentimental, or sickly but a broadside on to our experience. "I believe in God the Father almighty, maker of heaven and earth." But do you? Do I? Yes, but sometimes with a terrible struggle. When I read the newspaper, no day without a calamity of some kind, I want sometimes to cry out: "O God, why did you make all this?" But I know this, if we do not hold to this belief in God against all odds—yes, in the face of those two who found it in their hearts in Belfast recently to open fire indiscriminately in a pub full of people—if we do not hold fast to God as Creator, we are lost, we have no anchor at all, everything is futile, or in the words of Jean Paul Sartre, "Life is absurd."

Come down with me again to the foundations underneath all our church life as we know it. "I believe in God the Creator." Yes, but also this—"I believe in Jesus Christ."

And the belief is sharp and clear. It implies that what we know of the mind and character and purpose of God is spread out before us as if it were on a table. Jesus was a man. He lived as we lived. He had to eat, drink, wash, clean his teeth, and brush his hair. And the measure of our shock when I put it like this is the indication of how reluctant we are to recognize Jesus as a man. But he was. The creed even affirms that he suffered, died, and was buried as a man. That is to say he went through the whole range of our experience, boyhood, youth, manhood; and then pain, agonizing pain in the cruelest form of execution yet invented. All that life is spread out as it were on a table for us to see. Why? Because in that life and in that death and in the Resurrection too, what God is and what God does is exhibited.

No, I am not denying that God is experienced in the loveliness of nature, in music, poetry, yes, even in science, but only partially and in broken accents. It is into the face of Jesus Christ that we must look if we would see God as he really is. This is the foundation on which the church is built. This is what lies underneath all we see on top if we dig right down—"I believe in Jesus Christ," who loved me and gave himself for me.

Once more we dig—what do we find? "I believe in the Holy Spirit." But suppose I didn't. Suppose you didn't. Suppose the church didn't. What difference would it make? I'll tell you—the fossilization of the gospel. If we did not believe in the Holy Spirit, we should have to say, Oh, yes, maybe God created the World. If we did not believe in the Holy Spirit we should have to say, Oh, yes, Jesus was the finest type of manhood ever known, pity I didn't live in Palestine two thousand years ago to meet him. But because we believe in the Holy Spirit we believe that God is sustaining the universe now and is at work in the lives of people *today* lifting them up and transforming them sometimes with astonishing results.

A little while ago I visited one of the colleges in Oxford to meet five students. They had written to me offering their services in the Christian mission. What I found were three young men and two young women, all of them from non-church-going homes, whose lives had been completely altered by responding to the Christian gospel and who now had nothing to do with the promiscuity, rebellion, and experimentation with drugs so common with that age group; instead they were looking for ways of serving the community. So is Christianity a museum piece? Is it not a living force which changes people? Because people can be changed, whatever the critics may say.

Dig down then, and at the foundation level you will find this. "I believe in the Holy Spirit, *the author and giver of life,*" turning the historical into a present reality, changing people and changing circumstances.

Let me close with a question. Do you think the church will survive the next fifty years? Do you think it will stand up to all the changes that are bound to come, some of which we see beginning to operate already? But it has already survived two thousand years. What is more, it has survived in Russia after sixty years of the most scientific outrooting policy that has ever been put into practice, and today there is said to be more churchgoing in Russia than in Great Britain. What is essential for a building to stand? A good foundation. A foundation which cannot be moved. A foundation well laid in events in which God himself took a hand.

> I believe in God, maker of heaven and earth,
> I believe in Jesus Christ,
> I believe in the Holy Spirit—the Trinity,

for the future, and why we shall be wise to ally ourselves with that building called the church. "The rain came down, the floods rose, the wind blew, and beat upon that house; but it did not fall, because its foundations were on rock."

JOHN FRY

Blindness

Isaiah 40:1-8   Mark 10:46-52

Please ask no up-to-date questions of the great account of
the deliverance of Bartimaeus from his blindness, which is
not an up-to-date account. Do not say, "Was it a disease of
the eye? Did Jesus do the first corneal transplant? Was
Bartimaeus psychosomatically blind, perchance, his physical blindness caused by emotional illness?" These are
smart questions, all right, but the wrong questions, and
questions the Mark account provides no answers for.
Instead, try to stand down nineteen centuries to another
world view held by another people in another land. Listen
to the story the way the story was told.

Jericho was a walled city. On a main road of Palestine.
Bartimaeus seated himself outside the gate of the city in
order to present himself in his afflicted condition to the
numerous people using the road, hence coming into or
just leaving the city. He depended on pennies from
travelers. Pitiful pennies. Pennies dropped because of
pity. And he advertised his blindness by wailing. Poor
blind man whose every day was spent in arousing token
gifts from travelers. The people of the city, of course, who
knew him, his history, his father, his family, did not pity
him because they saw him every day and, as the residents
of the city knew, he could get around pretty well. He had
memorized the streets, knew where to turn, could find his

way. In the classic way of people who every day rub up against evil conditions, the citizens of Jericho ceased to care, to be horrified by blindness. He could die of hunger, and they would accuse him of lack of initiative.

So there sat Bartimaeus, just outside the city, begging from travelers, wailing out, "Help the blind man." He sat with the other derelicts, the other beggars. Now, Bartimaeus had heard that the great healer was in Jericho and hoped that Jesus would come on the road out of Jericho because he would at least make a good hit on Jesus. Popular figure. Popular figures and candidates, then as now, are not able to afford to pass up beggars. They tend to have to perform generously. When, according to his estimation, the noise he heard just inside the city kept coming nearer him, and he got it confirmed by the nonblind derelicts that it was in fact Jesus, Bartimaeus set up a super-wailing. A tremendous racket. "Jesus, Son of David, have mercy on me!" Over and over again. At the top of his lungs. Over the wailing of the other beggars. Over the noise of the people around Jesus. Clear, unmistakably louder and more hearable than the noise. This was an impertinent wailing. Uppity. A breach of the unspoken contract between beggars and beggees: namely, that beggars be demure, their faces to the ground, not overdoing it, otherwise beggees will be offended, stick their noses in the air and put their camels in low, and take off. So when Bartimaeus began his super-wailing, there were lots of people who started to shush him up. His fellow beggars, directly, and all of Israel, indirectly, who demand that beggars remain who they are and stay in the charity position, which is on their knees, quietly moaning. To all of these efforts to shush him up, to get him to remember who he was, for goodness' sake, Bartimaeus yelled louder, "Son of David, have mercy on me!" So what happened? Bartimaeus' bad tactics worked. Jesus did hear this one piercing voice over the general loud noise. Jesus instantly understood, as any Jew would, this breach of the charity situation. And maybe for a minute was stunned by that whole scene. These human wrecks. The legless, the diseased, the blind, absolutely depending for their very lives on the whimsical pennies of travelers because the people inside the city were too callous, too used to the obvious human suffering to care for them. The charity game. These misfits and maladepts, these wrecks having to prostrate themselves with quiet wailing before travelers in order merely and barely to survive. Thus half in anger he stopped and asked a disciple to produce the man. The bad tactic had worked. The beggars next to him told Bartimaeus the people were coming after him. He threw off his burnoose and met them half way, with the dignity of the blind walking unassisted across well-known territory. Their one remaining dignity. Pay attention to this blind man as he rises up and walks toward the people coming after him. Across ground he has never seen, among voices coming from people he has never seen, under a sun he has never seen, outside a city he has never seen; he has since birth lived a private history. He has had to depend on others to tell him what has happened. He has had to depend on their eyes and yet has come to believe that these on whom he is dependent have not told him all that they see, but rather what they want him to know. If he depends on them alone, his view of the outside world, of life itself, will be warped, screened, censored, half a world, and that half the crazy half. Those who aid the blind tend to believe the blind are somehow also stupid since they accept any story. By his wits he has lived, by his sharpened wits. He would have to believe the world full of the hardhearted and the condescending. A true hustler, who, had he not been an expert, could not have survived. As he picks his way so carefully, with such exaggerated dignity, he represents all of the derelicts of the earth, turned into hustlers by the hard hearts of their fellows; and more, he represents all who cannot see, who live on the piecemeal reports of others, so biased, so screened, and distorted, and as such live in private worlds instead of public worlds. He represents all who have blocked vision. They cannot see into things, or into people, or into the meaning of events. He becomes many people in those dramatic steps.

The blind Bartimaeus represented what the prophets called blindness, which had nothing to do with the physiological condition of the eyes but was, much more profoundly, a refusal to see, a stubbornness when it came to seeing. Blindness was hard eyes, evil eyes, which saw right through the plight of the poor as though they suddenly were invisible, which saw a representative of God as a trouble-maker who should be killed. The blind Bartimaeus was blindness itself coming toward Jesus. He stopped. In those seconds it had taken him to come before Jesus, the entire human situation had been excavated, revealing the shape of charity, the dereliction in being blind and a beggar, and the blindness of everyone standing there watching Bartimaeus. So this representative from the side of blindness met this representative from the side of deliverance. Jesus did *not* first ask him how long he had been blind. Jesus did *not* reach into his purse and extract an especially large gift, which is the very thing he might have done. He instead asked simply, "What do you want me to do for you?" Bartimaeus could not see Jesus, his eyes. But Bartimaeus had grown skilled in listening to voice inflections. He heard no money in the voice, no condescension, no charity. So Bartimaeus lifted up the heaviest words in his vocabulary, trembling with the strain of hoping. The big super-wailer suddenly could do no more than mumble. He had no experience in hoping. He had never said these words to himself, much less out loud and to anyone. But out they came: "Teacher let me receive my sight." Once said, there was no waiting, no dramatic period when Jesus evaluated them, evaluated his worthiness. As soon said, it was done. With a mighty rush from the side of deliverance, the words were spoken with the laughter of pure ecstasy, as Bartimaeus began his laughing with ecstasy, his running around, and shouting, and jumping up into the air, not being able to believe that he could see. He looked, and pointed, and peered, and reveled in color, shapes, gradations, the slants, the roughs, his eyes trying to exhaust the infinite novelty of the total landscape, seeing more in ten seconds than most seeing people see in a lifetime.

And so a great and mighty deliverance took place outside the city of Jericho, which had consigned Bartimaeus to everlasting blindness. Please do not single out this one deliverance. It fits within a pattern of accounts. Jesus had delivered people from insanity, paralysis, leprosy, suppurating wounds, deformity, and muteness. Each act of deliverance was symbolic because it demonstrated his sad cry for the plight of all permanently hopeless people in Palestine, and like bolts of lightning these acts of deliverance illuminated the ugliness of man to man. And these mighty acts of deliverance reveal the divine repugnance with the way things are. Every deliverance at the same time a judgment on the hard hearts of Israel. Every deliverance at the same time an excavation of Israel. Every deliverance at the same time an excavation of the human plight.

This Jesus, this King Jesus, this Lord Jesus, this Jesus Christ whose name we use to adorn our prayers, was a mighty man. His might lay in being able to see the textures of misery that everyone else passed right over. The miracle was that he looked across a beggar and was stunned into outrage at the sight, while the rest of mankind passed over such sights or began searching around for a suitably small coin to give the man—if, of course, he was clever in begging for it.

It is in just such a context we ought to read the commission report on civil disorders. It highlights more than all else the inability of America to conceive, even, the plight of the urban poor. America cannot see the charity situation for what it is. The situation of police brutality for what it is. The story of the deliverance of Bartimaeus should be required reading before you read the commission report. Then you have background to understand its insistence that there is a fundamental blindness in the land. Not merely an unwillingness but an inability to see the rank disparity in the living situations of the poor to the rich. Especially the black poor. All that can be said about the plight of Bartimaeus can be transferred exactly and said exactly of the members of the Welfare Tenants Unions who spoke with such eloquence yesterday as they testified before Illinois Lawmakers down in Springfield. They talked about the enforced patterns and degradation built into our charity system.

These derelicts were accepted by Jesus, therefore, as models of the deeper misery which afflicts mankind; in the instance of Bartimaeus, the deeper blindness. Our deeper blindness: an affliction of the spirit, some deformity of affection, some crippled courage, hidden agonies, all of them, hidden behind our flashing eyes and brilliant talk. But I hope you have understood, all along, this description of blindness can go very far toward describing the fundamental blindness of all those who do not see the plight of the actually blind and who invent these charity situations. Blindness is fundamentally reciprocal.

Forever seeking Jesus in the religious places and then missing him and his mighty deliverance. Seeking him among the crosses and candles. Not there. On the road with Bartimaeus, and if we cry hard enough and assault him with sufficient impertinence there, and these great blindnesses of ours are brought before him and we are actually delivered from their clutching power, then be prepared to meet him at this communion table. Amen.

JOHN N. GLADSTONE

Confidence for the Day of Judgment

That we may have confidence for the day of judgment.

—I John 4:17 RSV

I heard Dr. Murdo Ewen MacDonald, the distinguished Scottish preacher, relate the following story. During an American preaching tour, he felt constrained to give a message in one stately, prosperous church on the theme of judgment, the judgment of Christ. It was a solemn, searching message. Afterward, when the congregation lined up to shake hands with the preacher, one attractive, elegant lady held both his hands warmly, and said: "Gee, I guess you're real cute."

As a response to a sermon on judgment, that comment clearly left much to be desired. Perhaps, unwittingly, it expressed what so many inside and outside the church feel about the whole conception of our ultimate accountability to God. Treat it lightly, casually—even with amusement, lofty disdain, or supercilious skepticism. It is, after all, only an archaic hang-over from more primitive and credulous times. The old-time preachers used to take people by the scruff and hold them over the pit of hell until the smell of fire and brimstone choked them into repentance and faith. Not any longer! Educated preachers, like Alexander Pope's "Soft Dean," never mention hell to ears polite. God is love—which means benign, indulgent, cozy, and grandmotherly.

The truth is that we are right to jettison some of the awful, unbiblical, and almost sadistic concepts of judgment that were once clamorously proclaimed. Former generations tended to interpret with a lurid and unimaginative literalism the symbolic nature of our present knowledge of things unseen and eternal. They presumed to know too much about "the furniture of heaven and the temperature of hell." No doubt they were trying to communicate the urgency of the gospel invitation—a good fault!—but so often they conveyed the idea that they were trying to frighten people into the kingdom of God.

We must avoid the mistake of taking the pictorial, symbolic language of Scripture *literally*. We must also avoid the greater mistake of not taking it *seriously*. The judgment of God is a great inevitable reality. Let no one deride it. Let no one forget it. Let no one deny it. The day of judgment, the judgment of a holy God, demands our closest and reverent attention.

1.

"From thence he shall come to judge the living and the dead." Those words in the historic Apostles' Creed, recited by countless men and women across the centuries, are supported by a threefold witness.

There is *the witness of the reason*. The Greeks had no Bible, but they believed in judgment, calling it Nemesis. Why? Why, in generation after generation, have poets, philosophers, prophets, affirmed their belief in an ultimate day of judgment? Because the rationality of the world required it. If there is no judgment to come, then there is no moral law, order, or purpose in life, and conscience has no meaning. We live in chaos, in a world where crime pays, sin is an empty word, and everyone does that which is right in his own eyes. The ground plan of the universe is unreasonable if we are not accountable moral beings. Doesn't your mind make that affirmation? It is true that there is a process of judgment in life and history. This is so in the lives of individuals and nations. If they sow in sin, they reap in disaster; if they sow the wind, they reap the whirlwind. But not always in this life. Our minds demand a final accountability, a judgment that corrects the injustices of life.

There is *the witness of the Bible.* If the idea of a future day of judgment is to be discarded, then we must tear out whole pages of the Bible. Prophet, psalmist, and apostle sound the note over and over again. "If you seek him, he will be found of you: if you forsake him, he will cast you off forever." "It is appointed unto men once to die, but after this the judgment." "We must all appear before the judgment seat of Christ, and everyone of us shall give an account of himself before God." One could go on multiplying examples of such declarations in Scripture. It means that if the Bible is our authority, the Source Book of our holy faith, then everyone of us ought to be searching our hearts and asking earnestly:

> When Thou, my Righteous Judge, shall come
> To fetch Thy ransomed people home,
>   Shall I among them stand?

There is *the witness of Jesus himself.* He who was kindness incarnate, who spoke the loveliest words the world has ever heard, Jesus, all compassion, who said "Come to me, all you who labor and are heavy-laden, and I will give you rest," did not hesitate to speak of judgment to come. He spoke of the broad way leading to destruction, of separating some to the right hand and some to the left, of saying to some: "Depart from me, you cursed: I never knew you." We cannot accept some of the sayings of Jesus and reject others because they displease us. In the name of reason, of Scripture, and of Jesus himself we must affirm: "From thence He shall come to judge the living and the dead." A preacher must declare to himself and to the world the whole counsel of God. As David Christie has put it: "Rest assured that preaching which has drifted away from divine judgment will inevitably produce superficial people, bored people, unresponsible people. So long as we are called upon to speak to sinful people, we must speak of righteousness and judgment. And when we fail so to speak, men deep down in their hearts know us to be traitors to the truth."

2.

But all this is not the gospel! Gospel means good news, and it is not good news to be reminded that we must give an account one day to a holy and righteous God. It is, in fact, the background of the gospel. Hear now the good news as John records it: "That we may have confidence for the day of judgment." Confidence! Not shivering in terror, not shrinking shame, but confident! Confident before the righteous Judge, the Sovereign God, the Eternal Throne! Incredible—but exhilarating, exalting, and gloriously true! "That we may have confidence for the day of judgment."

Let no one imagine that the reference here is to self-confidence, a confidence based on our own supposed merit or assumed superiority. That, I'm sorry to say, is a confidence that some Christians appear to have. We presume to judge the spiritual status of others—always to our own advantage. Jesus disposed of such spiritual arrogance in one devastating sentence: "Judge not, that you be not judged." Censorious judgment of our fellows is simply not the human stance.

The grounds of our confidence on the day of judgment are not in ourselves. Far from it! John expounds them for us in this letter. They are in Christ!

> On Christ the solid rock, we stand
> All other ground is sinking sand.

The first ground of our confidence is in *our belief in Christ*. John writes in verse 15: "Whoever confesses that Jesus is the Son of God, God abides in him, and he in God" (RSV). We can be confident when we meet Christ as Judge then if we have met Christ as Savior now. He will confess us as his friends before God the Father then, if we confess him as the Son of God before the world now. "What must I do to be saved?" may be an unfashionable question, but it is as vital as ever So is the answer: "Believe in the Lord Jesus, and you will be saved." What, then, does it mean to believe in Christ?

It certainly involves intellectual consent. For me to confess that Jesus is the Son of God is first an intellectual confession. Because of the historical evidence of the New Testament, the claims of Jesus himself and my own personal experience of his living presence, I can do no other. It commends itself to my mind. Of course it is more than intellectual consent. Of course, the mental capacities of us all vary considerably. There is such a thing as "simple faith." But let us be clear about this. Christianity has nothing to fear intellectually. It transcends reason, but it is never irrational. Examine the evidence yourself. Explore the tremendous fact of Christ. Like Thomas in the Gospel record you may well be compelled to fall at his feet and cry adoringly, "My Lord and My God."

It also involves total commitment. Belief is commitment, the total commitment of the whole personality to the Son of God as Savior and Lord; total commitment to him as One who bore our sins in his own sinless body, who took our place and our rightful judgment upon himself. It is one thing to believe about Christ. It is quite another to believe in Christ. A merely theoretical or traditional belief is not enough. Dr. T. F. Torrance tells how he sat in a hotel restaurant near a man who looked abjectly miserable and worried. Torrance spoke to him, and discovered that the man had served as a sailor in the first World War. His ship had been torpedoed off the coast of Africa. When they got into the boats, if was found that in his boat there was one too many, and they began to cast lots who should go overboard so that the rest, if possible, should be saved. But a young lad of only sixteen or seventeen years stood up and said: "I have no father and no mother, but Jesus Christ died for me, and I will gladly die for you." For years the picture of that act of self-sacrifice had haunted this old sailor, and behind it all the figure of the crucified Son of God who had died for us all. But he had persistently resisted the claims of Christ, who haunted his memories. He had tried to drive away the vision by drink, but was unable to shake off the haunting presence of the crucified. Now he was old—and Jesus Christ was still a haunting presence, not an accepted Savior and acknowledged Lord. To believe in Christ now, to be intellectually convinced and totally committed to him now, will be a sure ground of confidence for the day of judgment. "Whoever confesses that Jesus is the Son of God," the Son of God will confess before his Father in Heaven.

The second ground of our confidence is *our union with Christ*. John writes, in verse 16: "He who abides in love abides in God" (RSV). This thought takes us beyond belief to the idea of a mystical union with Christ, living in close, intimate fellowship with him as he lives in us by his Spirit, the Spirit of love.

It is a personal union, closer and more personal than any union we can know. In practical terms it means cultivating his presence daily, sharing our lives with him through thought and prayer, letting him refine our natures, mold our character, forgive our sins, heal our wounds. It is well known that two people who love each other very much tend to grow like each other. Abiding, dwelling in love, they grow together. So Christ, who loves us and whom we love, gradually changes us into his own likeness as we say, "I am his and he is mine." We are conformed to his image. The Judge we shall meet at the end is the familiar friend of each returning day!

It is also a social union. We do not abide in Christ alone. United with him, we are united with all who share our love and his risen presence. This means the fellowship of the church, his Body. What brings us together and holds us together in the church, with all our likes and dislikes and enormous differences, is our common share in Christ. We love one another because Christ loves in us and through us. We help, inspire, encourage, and strengthen one another in Christ. And the climax of this union, its visible expression, is the Lord's Supper, the Communion Service, where we eat the bread and drink the cup, feeding on Christ by faith with thanksgiving—until he comes again! A friend of mine has described a most moving Communion service he shared in one Christmas Eve, as a prisoner of war. Morale was at a low ebb. There was no fuel, and the temperature was sub-zero. With hardly any food, the men were cold, hungry, and depressed. The Chaplain decided to hold a Christmas Eve Communion service, and appealed for bread. Six hundred men came, each carrying one slice of bread, one third of their rations! The whole service was charged with meaning and hope, with a sense of sacrifice, as together they cemented their union with Christ, and were nourished by him. "That we may have confidence for the day of judgment," we believe in Christ and live in union with Christ, together with all faithful people who find in Him their life, their health, their joy and peace.

The third ground of our confidence is *our conformity to Christ.* John says, in verse 17: "Because as he is so are we in this world" (RSV). "As he is so are we." That is, we are to be like him, to behave like him, to conform to his mind and purpose and will in the world. To be sure, we can never completely conform to him. He was sinless, morally perfect, utterly obedient always. But conformity to him, as we are able and enabled, is our goal.

This is an answer to those who think that faith in Christ is a cheap and easy indulgence, a cowardly escape from the consequences of our own sin. No! No! Believing in him, united with him, conforming to him is heart-searching, disturbing, challenging. It means obedience at all costs, service at all times, taking up our cross and following in his steps. Cheap and easy? It is the hardest thing in the world. Any fool can conform to the world. Millions do. There are people who drink alcohol, for example, because they are afraid to be different from some friends, or social set, craving the approval of others, fearing their ridicule. They will do anything, go anywhere—even renounce their faith—rather than risk unpopularity. In other words, such people are more concerned to conform to the world than to Christ, more concerned with the judgment of their friends than they are with the judgment of Christ. It is a curious and sad thing. What does the hollow laughter or bitter hostility of this world mean compared with the approval of One who loved us and gave himself for us, and before whose burning love we must all stand at last?

Conform to Christ! "As he is so are we." I am always deeply moved when I recall what happened to Samuel Logan Brengle, an American Methodist minister, in 1848. In that year, when William Booth's Salvation Army was enlisting men from all over the world, Brengle felt called to cross the Atlantic and offer his services. A successful minister in a fine church, he gave up everything in obedience to the call. At first, the general accepted him grudgingly and reluctantly. "You've been your own boss too long," he said. To instill humility in him, Booth set Brengle to work cleaning the boots of other trainees. Brengle said to himself, "Have I followed my own fancy across the Atlantic in order to black boots?" He had once dreamed of being a Bishop. He had given up so much! Then, as in a vision, he saw his Lord bending over the feet of rough, unlettered fishermen—and washing their feet! "Lord," he whispered, "you washed their feet; I will black their boots." "As he is so are we." Conformity to Christ!

I walked once with a friend down a busy road, and we saw a man with a doleful expression slowly parading up and down, carrying a poster bearing the words: "Prepare to meet thy God." It seemed to me a foolish way of witnessing, and I said: "How awful! Trying to threaten people!" My friend replied: "You interpret those words as a threat. I see them as a glorious hope. How marvelous to meet our God—the God of Creation, of Jesus, of love and mercy! I'm prepared, excited!" The point was well taken. We must all meet God at last. It may seem a threatening prospect—the weak before the Omnipotent, the sinful before the holy, the mortal before the infinite. But God has already met us! Rich in mercy, boundless in compassion, he has taken the initiative to give us grounds for confidence on the day of meeting.

> O loving wisdom of our God.
> When all was sin and shame,
> A second Adam to the fight
> And to the rescue came.

The second Adam is Christ! And by our belief in Christ, our union with Christ, our conformity to Christ "we may have confidence for the day of judgment."

PETER J. GOMES

Thinking Hearts and Loving Minds

Lessons: Mark 12:28-34 and Romans 12:1-21

On Friday last, we engaged in one of our familiar rituals here: members of this university gathered in Memorial Church to pay respects to one of its most distinguished citizens and sons, Kirtley Fletcher Mather, professor of geology, emeritus, who died in the ninetieth year of his age. There were few undergraduates present: they were busy about the business of living: scurrying off to class or lunch, in contemplation of or contention with the world of tomorrow's possibilities. But those hundred or more souls who gathered here, students, colleagues, family, and friends of Kirtley Mather, they were for a few moments in a season of suspended time. It was a happy time and a happy service, almost as happy as the day, but eighteen months ago, in this very place, when Professor Mather, at age ninety-nine, took another wife, and in answer to the inevitable but still impertinent question, "Why?" responded: "She was lovely, and I was lonely." At year's end, that wedding was listed as one of the year's "Ten Best Events" by the Boston *Phoenix*. This was a day of a different character but the same joy. Professor Stephen Jay Gould of the geology department remarked in his brief tribute that Kirtley Mather was one of the two professors in his whole academic experience whom he both loved and respected: his qualities of mind and heart were sufficient to endear him to a man barely half his age. These were qualities, however, that were not displayed in abstraction or isolation: the usual rigorous mind in the classroom, the affectionate heart at home. It was the totality, the integrity, the wholeness of the man in which these qualities of mind and heart shone as a single identity which made him such a singular person and produced so singular an impression: a quality all too rarely found in our university today, and more the pity, for in some sense such a quality, embodied in human beings in the heroic search for truth, is the essence of what an education and a university are. And so we laid Kirtley Mather to rest with his ancestors, and yet those qualities which made him so remarkable in life and memorable in death continue to both entice and elude us who are still in our pilgrimage. How, we ask, can we balance our feelings with our knowledge? What does passion have to say to competence? How does the Christian, and the Christian scholar and student in particular, juggle the tender relationships between the demands of the heart and of the mind?

When I was a freshman in college, my classmates and I in freshman speech were assigned the memorization of certain passages from Edmund Burke for presentation in class. As we were called upon at random by Professor Quimby, one of my classmates declined to recite the passage assigned, and addressing the professor and class, announced that she had prayed upon the matter at hand and the Lord had laid upon her a message of a different sort to give us, which she did: in the hushed silence that followed her remarkable testimonial, we waited for the response of Professor Quimby. He considered himself for a moment and then said, "Madam, as God is not taking this course for credit, I dare not evaluate the truth of what he has had to say to you; you are, however, and you fail." And here fell one more victim of the heart to the mind. Illustrations such as this, of which there are legion in all our academic closets, are sufficient to remind us that inspiration, especially divine inspiration, has little to do with instruction, and that the heart of religion and the mind of human knowledge have very little to do with one another: they should maintain a polite but indifferent acquaintance, lest feeble faith be corrupted or strong intellect undermined.

Thus, when one encounters in one person qualities of mind and spirit that transcend the caricature of either, one is surprised, grateful, and not a little suspicious. But what we are speaking of here is a tradition of wholeness—no, more than a tradition: an *ideal* of wholeness that goes to the heart of our identity as Christians and Jews and from which we have departed only since the relatively modern period of the enlightenment. The wholeness of all experience, the relatedness of all knowledge, which in its proper perspective is wisdom, was the business of philosophic inquiry from the earliest thinkers onward. Long before philosophy became mere verbal mathematics, philosophers were anxious to understand that larger context in which both heart and mind played their part. But such sadly is not the case today: there is a sense in which heart and head are regarded as mutually exclusive and indeed as antagonists, and a sign of maturity is the necessary but painful struggle to choose between the two and pledge one's lifelong allegiance to that choice. This struggle certainly takes place in life, and it takes place with a particular vengeance in the church, which might be thought to have transcended the whole debate. The reason indeed that my predecessors as preachers to the university were endowed on the Plummer Foundation was Miss Caroline Plummer's notion in 1958 that Harvard then had enough "professors of the head" and that what was now needed was a "professor of the heart," of the "pneumatic experience of religion." And we who have sat in her chair have ever since borne that unfortunate distinction in this university as professors of feelings rather than thoughts. Her intentions were of the best, however, and she sought to restore the broken balance between these two qualities by providing for the weaker and neglected part.

The difficulty is, however, that the very provision, necessary though it was, and is, serves to accentuate the dangerous and destructive notion that these are two combative and competitive modes of inquiry that require, like rival political parties, equal time, so that the discerning might make better informed choices. Our tradition suggests that such neat packaging is neither necessary nor even possible if our vision of the person is greater than the sum of its parts.

Indeed, both of the lessons from Scripture read for us by John Nichols and Louise Senior suggest that God is not satisfied with less than the whole being, the total sum of his creation and our existence. The summary of the law makes that unavoidably clear: thou shalt love the Lord thy God with all thy *heart,* with all thy *soul,* with all thy *mind,* and with all thy *strength.* And again, in that wonderful twelfth chapter of Romans, in the New English translation, "I implore you by God's mercy to offer your very selves to him: a living sacrifice, dedicated and fit for his acceptance, the worship offered by mind and heart" (NEB). It should be clear to us that from the beginning, these gifts of God, the mind and the heart, the capacities to feel and understand, are both required by God if we are to come to know him, love him, and serve him. They are not mutually exclusive, one supportive of and the other subserving to faith: and both must take their part in the larger enterprise of faith by which the Christian moves, both in classroom and in chapel. But to say that and that alone is to leave us with that familiar though unexamined feeling of well-being so dangerous to the religious mind when hard questions are put. And the hard question, so frequently put around here by old and young alike, but particularly by the young is this: How do I relate what I know to what I feel? How can I make sense of my feelings, and what is the proper relationship between the two? What adjustments must I make in order simply to survive?

Professor Gould remarked that he used to invite Professor Mather to lecture in his natural science class once a year, which he did until a very few years ago. The geological lecture hall was filled with undergraduates as they heard this old man talk about the Scopes trial, in which he gave evidence, and his resultant friendship both with Scopes and Darrow; and they would be fascinated with his discussions of the technical study of geology and the development of that science as he had seen it for nearly seventy years. And then, at the end of his lecture, he would give a little discourse on the moral uses of knowledge and how science was a part of both the moral and spiritual foundations of the universe, a gift, as it were, to the understanding, and of how we should approach such knowledge on reverent feet. In the late sixties, students used to be rather condescending toward the old man for these rather antediluvian views; they would listen politely, but were much more interested in the hard stuff with which he had presented them earlier. In the early seventies, however, while the hard stuff had lost none of its appeal, it was the concluding spiritual wisdom which had the undergraduates straining to catch every word. His credentials as a scientist were impeccable, and yet he found more than these needful; and he was willing to share that need with yet another generation. Could it be that their tolerance had turned to neediness, the sense that in a world going madder every day, any clue toward hope and meaning would be gratefully accepted? Perhaps they too were looking for that ultimate alchemy whereby mere hearts and minds become transformed into living souls, and if they were, they would be joining the pilgrimage of the ages.

But what kind of hearts and minds are these that would be worthy of our loyalty and of a community such as this? Not long ago, I was present at the installation of a college chaplain in a place where there hadn't been one before. In former days, it was assumed that the business of religion and the life of the spirit was everybody's business; but now, the college had come of age, and it was determined that as in every field, religion now belonged to the professional, and so one was hired. In the charge given to my new colleague, he was reminded that he would only be able to minister to that place if he loved it with his mind and thought about it with his heart. In the whole perfunctory service it was the one thought that stayed with me;

89

obviously, it impressed me enough to try it on you, but even more than that, it defined so well what I feel is my relationship to you and this community in the Lord, and what I feel is your duty to your faith and this community in the Lord: to love with the mind and to think with the heart—thinking hearts and loving minds. There is room in the mind for passion, and there is room in the heart for perseverance, and there is necessity for both for Christ's sake, and our own.

Let me say a word about passion in the mind. There is a scholarly article, complete with footnotes, entitled "Harvard Indifference" (*NEQ,* September, 1976), which traces the development of this stereotypical lack of enthusiasm through the writers and literature associated with this place. Professor Hedrick's fascinating article only confirms what all of us have always known, and what I fear new students, here less than a month, have perhaps already absorbed into their bloodstream: that it is not cool to be hot, about anything or anybody. Original sin here is to be "too anything," lest someone think you are enthusiastic; and that, we know since the eighteenth century, is an intellectual "fox pass" of the worst order. I have told you before of the elegant inscription on the tomb of the Countess of Huntington, just outside Winchester, in England, which reads, to the effect:

She was a Godly, righteous, and sober Lady, bounteous in good works and Christian affections, a firm believer in the Gospel of our Lord and Saviour Jesus Christ, and devoid of the taint of enthusiasm.

To be "enthused" in those days was to be mad; to be enthused in more recent history is to set oneself up for a terrific fall; and thus, for self-preservation, the objective distance is to be cultivated. Henry Adams in his *Education,* which is somewhat ours as well, knew that the Harvard student's greatest weakness was lack of passion of the mind: He wrote: "Afraid of serious risks, and still more afraid of personal ridicule, he seldom made a great failure of life, and nearly always led a life more or less worth living."

What a joy: to lead a life "more or less worth living." Enriching the Brahmin blood by frequent transfusions from the West has not overcome that tendency toward the safe and the sure, but perhaps for some it has unlocked the passions of the mind where information becomes knowledge, and knowledge wisdom, and wisdom grace and excitement. The discoveries that illuminate us in the laboratory or the stacks, in the concert at Sanders or the play at the Loeb, or in a quiet walk through Mt. Auburn or along the river: these are things of which the mind's passion is made, and these are the gifts which God gives to starved and sheltered minds if we will only open ourselves to receive them. Passion has to do with love: not just feeling, but real, deep, penetrating, abiding love: and love, as we all know, is full of risks and dangers and disappointments. Robert Frost described himself as having a lover's quarrel with the world. He cared enough for who and where he was that he never rested from his labors until his labors were ended: his tools were the pen; his resource, the mind; his agenda, the heart. To be passionate, you have got to care; the thinking heart accepts nothing less.

But passion alone is early and frequently spent. Thinking hearts, yes, but loving minds as well. There is room in the mind for passion, but there is room in the heart for perseverance as well. Perseverance is hardly thought of as a romantic virtue. It is scarcely sudden or enflamed; it does not pulsate with action or evident accomplishment. And yet, without it, the heart is really just so much sentiment. If you think with your heart, you have to have the capacity to persevere, because the heart sets such extraordinary goals, goals beyond the measure of the mind that it is only in persistent toil that those goals can be brought nearer to accomplishment. This is a lesson those who would invest their hearts in the righteous causes of our age and place need to remember. We are all impatient for justice, here, in South Africa, everywhere. Many of you felt that the cause of justice in South Africa was unnecessarily delayed by the President and Fellows' decision concerning divestiture in companies doing business in South Africa. Some of you argued: "We gave them truth, and they gave us 'no.'" The heart and the mind tell us that we are offended by such an action, that the world cannot wait until we have persuaded everyone concerned of the justness of our cause and the propriety of our course. All this may well be true: but the heart has more lessons to teach us about persistence than we are perhaps willing to hear. Change does not happen abracadabra: when it does, as in a hurricane or natural disaster, it is termed an "act of God" by the insurance people. Human change is manifest only after frequently anonymous and always persistent efforts in the face of apparently insurmountable obstacles. . . . It is in the interests of most human institutions to resist change, including the corporation and the church. It is the duty of those of us who care for those institutions and for the world in which they are set to persevere in our efforts of the heart, not because we expect to see the victory in our time and terms, but because the effort is worth making.

Now, where is the gospel, where is the good news in all of this business about heart and mind, passion and persever-ance, indifference and enthusiasm? The mind and the heart are the gifts of God: we did not create them, nor can we get on well without them. But lest we think of them as mere abstractions, polar opposites useful for comparative purposes alone, he has also given us Jesus Christ, in whom the thinking heart and the loving mind are found in their most profound human form: Jesus whose heart made him weep at the loss of his friend Lazarus, and whose one passion, his involvement with the cares and wounds of the world, took him to the cross for our sake; Jesus, whose mind disputed with the doctors in the temple and who persevered in love then and now in the face of hostility, indifference, and ridicule, living and losing his life, that our life might be more than "mere living." When God calls us to holiness, to whole-ness, which I believe he does here and now, he calls us to the largest possible view, from which nothing and no one is excluded. He calls this church, even this college, and surely this world, to such a visionary reunion of heart and mind, passion and perseverance, that should we accept his invitation so freely given, only God alone could imagine the kind of world in which we would dwell. There comes a time when the fractured whole of heart and mind yearn for reunion, that what God had intended for us may now by his grace be accomplished. Perhaps this is the time and even the place when that wholeness for which we seek may come to pass. God grant that it may be so.

What we have heard with our ears and said with our lips, may we take to our hearts and show forth in our lives, for Christ's sake. Amen.

WILLIAM E. HULL

Prayer: Human and Divine

Romans 8:26-27

No wonder Paul turned to prayer at this point! Having led his readers to the brink of a cosmic abyss, the Apostle there surveyed a vast panorama of suffering, frustration, and futility that not only engulfed the whole of mankind but convulsed the church as well. Caught in the cleft of a fractured universe, writhing in travail as a new age of freedom came to birth, even spirit-filled Christians groaned inwardly as they waited in hope for a deliverance yet to be completed (Rom. 8:18-25).

Responding to the paradox of Christian existence, which was, in turn, rooted in the anguish of the human situation, Paul sketched the profoundest conception of prayer in all of Scripture (Rom. 8:26-27). Standing on the spiritual summit which we identify as Romans 8, he dared to relate our stammering sighs to the very dialogue within the Godhead itself. Each affirmation arrests our attention with startlingly unexpected truth. First the passage shatters prevailing assumptions about prayer, then it builds a breathtaking alternative to put in their place. Three convictions undergird this revolutionary breakthrough in our understanding of the ultimate basis of prayer.

I. The Human Problem

In our weakness, we cannot pray as God intends.

Surely Paul was not serious in the flat assertion, "We do not even know how we ought to pray" (v. 26b NEB). His

Bible was full of prayers, the Psalms including some of the choicest supplications in Hebrew history. He was raised in Pharisaism (Acts 23:6; 26:5; Phil. 3:5), the finest flowering of prayer piety in first-century Judaism. The early Christian movement was born in Pentecostal prayer (Acts 1:14, 24; 2:42; 3:1; 4:31) and was sustained by the unceasing prayers of its converts (e.g., I Thess. 5:17; II Thess. 1:11; Col. 1:9). As a leading scholar of this passage has complained, the principle "that Christian prayer never really knows anything about God's will or what its own content ought to be . . . is simply absurd, and contradicts everything that the New Testament has otherwise to say on the subject."[1]

On the contrary, Paul's disconcerting insistence on a "weakness" that flaws even our finest efforts to pray is rooted at the very center of Scripture, for he learned this radical truth from his Lord. The Sermon on the Mount leveled a sweeping indictment against the prayer practices of both "hypocrites" and "heathen" (i.e., Jews and Gentiles)—which, together, included the leaders of all known religions! Prevailing patterns were so corrupted by mixed motives and empty phrases that Jesus dared to insist, "Don't pray like that!" (Matt. 6:5-8). In the parable of the pharisee and the publican, he depicted the former as a virtuoso in the fine art of public praying, but then rejected his prayer, which was a model by human standards; instead, he chose to exalt the latter, whose only accomplishment was to show conclusively that he knew nothing about how to pray! (Luke 18:9-14.)[2]

Jesus cherished no illusions regarding the ability even of his own disciples to frame worthy petitions. When two of his closest, James and John, came with their hearts' deepest desire, he swept aside the request with a shattering rejoinder, "You do *not* know what you are *asking*" (Mark 10:38a RSV). Even though his followers had long since learned to pray from Scripture and synagogue, some even from John the Baptist, they glimpsed an intensity and profundity to his own prayer life

95

which caused them to plead, "Lord, teach us to pray" (Luke 11:1 RSV). In response, Jesus gave them an example so uniquely his own that to this day we still call it not our but "The *Lord's* Prayer." It is his not simply by virtue of authorship but because, instinctively, we realize that *we* do not know how to pray like that!

Beyond all of this, there was one awful moment when the truth of our text was burned unforgettably into Christian memory. "Watch and pray," he had urged his inner circle as they entered with him upon that climactic vigil in Gethsemane. Thrice he summoned them to urgent intercession, and thrice they succumbed to the stupor of sleep (Mark 14:37-41). How tragic was their spiritual dereliction! Little could they realize that prayer was intended to arm them for that tragic battlefield called Calvary where the great tribulation would soon rage. Here, at the moment when Christ's followers were counted on to pray as never before, the stark reality was forever exposed that even the best of them abysmally failed even though it was an imperative necessity!

It is not a long journey from Gethsemane back to our text in Romans. The Pauline insistence that, despite the help of the Spirit *(pneuma),* we live in "weakness" *(asthenia)* echoes the verdict of Jesus in the garden that "the spirit *[pneuma]* indeed is eager but the flesh is weak *[asthenēs],*" nowhere more so than at the point of our inability to pray (Mark 14:38). We would like to concede only that our *outer* life is weak because of the limitations of the "flesh," whereas our *inner* life is strong because of the indwelling of the Spirit. But the Apostle refused to adopt that view popularized by Pietism. Instead, he insisted that it was deep within, at the innermost core of our being where we pray, that the painful sense of helplessness is most acute. Tension and contradiction run to the very roots of life (cf. II Cor. 6:8-10). Ignorance infects even the impulse to pray (cf. I Cor. 13:9). Groanings issue from the holy of holies itself (cf. Rom. 8:23)!

And the irony of it all is that prayer is not some option which we may abandon because of our "weakness" but is a necessity mandated by the will of God for each Christian life. Everything Paul said in Romans 7 makes prayer imperative, while everything he said in Romans 8 makes it inevitable. Imperative because sin and death are still at work in our lives, because the will is unable to carry out its highest resolves, because our wretchedness cries out for redemption (Rom. 7:13-25). Inevitable because we are now free from condemnation, because we now live by the Spirit, because we are children of God (Rom. 8:1-17). Paul has sharpened the paradox to its breaking point by juxtaposing the weakness of man, which makes true prayer impossible, with the will of God, which makes it essential. The very thing that we do *not* know how to do is the very thing that we *must* do "just as God intends."[3] The crux of the dilemma is captured in this paraphrase: "Weak as we are, we do not know the way that God would have us pray, even though that kind of praying has become the deepest compulsion of our lives!"

It is still difficult in our day to admit the truth of this disturbing contention. Lurking in every religious breast is the glib assumption that, when all else is lost, at least we can pray. How easy it is to say grace before each meal or to repeat the Lord's Prayer by rote a thousand times over! Always there is some saint waiting in the wings to give triumphant testimony to the efficacy of prayer. To most people, praying is an intrinsically good activity as natural as breathing. Such simple faith is dismayed by the Pauline suggestion that we really do not know anything about prayer after all, except that it is beyond our reach.

How foolishly we deceive ourselves! Signs of our impotence in prayer abound on every hand. We were going to pray until the sinner's heart was melted and revival broke out in our midst—but we didn't! We resolved to maintain personal devotions and a family altar—but we didn't! We determined to uphold a missionary or a minister in our intercessions—but we didn't! The corpses of our dead prayer promises lie rotting all about us like victims of a plague. More prayer crusades have collapsed than any charitable historian would care to record. To the Master's question, "Could you not watch one hour?" (Mark 14:37), the answer, more often than not, is *no*. Why not admit what the Bible unblinkingly affirms—that we have not learned how to make prayer the channel of that spiritual wisdom and power for which we so desperately yearn?

At no time is this more true than when our paths wind through Gethsemane, those desperate moments when we seem utterly vulnerable to the onslaught of evil, when everything we cherish seems nailed to a cross. Illustrations abound. An eagerly awaited baby is born deformed, and the parents do not know whether to pray that he live or that he die. A marriage begets lovely children but somehow dies itself in the process, and the couple does not know whether to pray for a divorce that would tear the family circle asunder or for the preservation of a relationship that has become a living hell. A minister finds himself in an inflamed society not knowing whether to pray for a courage that would split his congregation or for a patience that would compromise his convictions. A scientist with a lethal new discovery that could destroy the world does not know whether to pray that his country develop it into a dangerous weapon or suppress it in the hope that enemy nations will never make the same discovery.

On and on the list might go, but the point is clear: "the sufferings of this present time" (v. 18) confront us with baffling ambiguities that call forth groans (v. 23) instead of answers. Caught up in the vast travail by which God is seeking to free his creation from corruption (vv. 21-22), we are sometimes left "with no language but a cry,"[4] much like the psalmist who, in his distress, "cried unto the Lord" (e.g., Psalm 107:6, 13, 19, 28); or, like our Lord, whose last act on the cross was to utter "a loud cry" (Matt. 27:50 and parallel Mark 15:37).[5] But once Paul forced this shattering recognition, he set beside it the incredible contention that precisely in that weakness, and in the groanings which it calls forth, we may discover help from none other than the Holy Spirit of God!

II. The Divine Provision

The Spirit shares our plight by interceding with inexpressible groanings.

If anything, Paul's notion that God's Spirit helps the weak "with groanings too deep for words" is even more incredible than his complementary notion of the Christian's inability to pray. For the concept of deity was very transcendent in the first century: God was holy, righteous, exalted. Except for limited foreshadowings in the Hebrew prophets (e.g., Hos. 11:8),[6] neither Judaism nor paganism knew anything about a God who groans. The very idea was a scandal, implying that the Sovereign of creation was somehow ensnared in the predicament of his creatures. Where, then, did Paul get this audacious belief in a Spirit who identifies with the deepest human agonies? Ultimately it came from the same source as his other convictions about prayer, the witness of his Lord, Jesus Christ.

The word-group for "groaning" occurs only twice in the Gospels. In Mark 7 they brought to Jesus a tongue-tied deaf-mute for healing. Laboring over the man's speech impediment with spittle, Jesus looked up into heaven and *groaned* (Mark 7:34). In Mark 8 the Pharisees came "seeking from him a sign from heaven," whereupon Jesus "*groaned* deeply in his spirit" and rejected their request (Mark 8:12). In both cases, here were men who could not ask for what they really needed, one because of a physical malady, the other because of a theological malady. And, in both cases, Jesus met their inability to ask aright with a groan! Such a reaction reflected not only his deep involvement in human misery but also the attitude of his heavenly Father toward those with wayward tongues.

But, once again, the climactic insight came in connection with Gethsemane. As they went forth to that garden vigil, Simon Peter, the fearless leader of the disciple band, had vowed a faithfulness unto death, only to be told by Jesus that his courage would collapse before morning

(Matt. 26:33-34 and parallels Mark 14:29-30 and Luke 22:33-34; cf. John 13:37-38). And, sure enough, his utter failure to claim the needed prayer power in Gethsemane quickly led to a threefold denial as cockcrow signaled the approaching sunrise (Matt. 26:69-75 and parallels Mark 14:66-72 and Luke 22:56-62). Yet all was not lost. For Jesus had already moved to deal with Peter's prayer poverty even before it was exposed in the garden. In the upper room, prior to the prediction of denial, he had solemnly announced: "Simon, Simon, behold, Satan demanded to have you that he might sift you like wheat, but *I have prayed for you* that your faith may not fail" (Luke 22:31-32 RSV).

This became the bedrock assurance on which our text is based, not that Christians prove to be heroes in every crisis but that Christ prays for his own. Two memories came from Gethsemane: one that the disciples were weak and thus slept when they should have been praying; the other that, as they slept, Jesus went a little farther and prayed with an agony beyond description. In place of this scene, the Gospel of John substituted the great high priestly prayer, which has as its centerpiece a magnificent section that begins, "*I am praying for them;* I am not praying for the world but for those whom thou hast given me" (John 17:9 RSV; emphasis added). The Epistle to the Hebrews also remembered Gethsemane, where "Jesus offered up prayers and supplications, *with loud cries* and tears" (5:7a RSV), but this historical memory was there translated into the theological conviction that "he is able *for all time* to save those who draw near to God through him, since *he always lives to make intercession for them*" (7:25 RSV).

With this rich legacy of faith from the life of his Lord, it is little wonder that Paul was made bold to describe in our text the Gethsemane of Christ's Spirit. Just as the Savior emptied himself by identifying with the sin of the world on a cross (Phil. 2:5-8), so the Comforter condescended to participate with Christians in their ongoing predicament. If they groan (Rom. 8:23), *he* groans (v. 26c), with this difference: the church groans because of its weakness and need of help, whereas the Spirit groans because of his intercession and willingness to help! It is not just that the Spirit guides us to pray aright, so that now all of our praying is "*in* the Spirit" (Eph. 6:18; Jude 20). Rather the spirit goes beyond even that by praying not only *through* us but also *on behalf of* us.

If the identification of the spirit *with us* leads to right words in prayer, from "Abba" to "Amen" (Rom. 8:15-16; Gal. 4:6; I Cor. 12:3; 14:16), then the intercession of the Spirit *for us* leads to groanings "too deep for words." At least two reasons account for this inarticulateness. The first is that the agenda concerns our most poignant agonies (v. 23), those "sufferings of this present time" (v. 18) for which the dictionaries of earth have no adequate terminology. The second is that the Spirit has such direct and immediate communion with the Father that no words are needed to build a bridge between them. What this speechless profoundity means in practical terms is that the spirit is helping us even when we cannot hear it, that prayer of the highest order is taking place amid those ceaseless strivings which we feel so deeply but cannot put into words.

If this be true, then the ultimate paradox is confirmed that where we are the weakest, there God's power is the strongest (cf. I Cor. 1:26-31). Elsewhere, Paul spoke of a revelation so exalted that he heard things "which man may *not utter,*" only to receive with it a "thorn in the flesh" so harassing that it left him in *"weakness."* The resolution of this intolerable tension came with the realization that God's power "is made perfect in weakness," so that when we are weak, precisely then we are strong (II Cor. 12:1-10). Again and again we have found it so. Earth's thorns prick and tear at heaven's visions until groans rise from the depths of our being. But even then—especially then!—we may dare to believe that the Spirit is adding *his* groans to our own and offering them at the throne of God!

III. The Ultimate Purpose

*God searches our hearts to discern the intention
of the Spirit's intercession.*

How is this intercession received by the Father in heaven? A classic Old Testament concept, often associated with prayer, was that God searches every human heart (I Sam. 16:7; Ps. 139:1-2; Prov. 15:11; Jer. 17:10) to discover those deepest secrets by which all are judged (I Kings 8:38-39; Ps. 7:9; 17:3; 26:2; 44:20-21). Paul gave this traditional idea fresh meaning by suggesting that God now looks in the hearts of Christians not for their good or evil thoughts but for "the mind of the Spirit" (v. 27*a*), i.e., his aims and aspirations in striving on our behalf. Nor is it hard for God to discern the intention of his own Holy Spirit. If the Father can ferret out the hidden deceptions of wayward creatures whose thoughts are not his thoughts (Isa. 55:8), how much more can he "know" with certainty the mind-set of one who is of his very Being. In I Cor. 2:10-11, Paul had said that the Spirit alone "comprehends the thoughts of God" because he "searches everything, even the depths of God." Now he affirmed the converse, that God alone comprehends the thoughts of the Spirit because he searches everything, even the depths of the Spirit.

And what does God find as a result of this search? Why, he finds what Paul had already affirmed in the previous verse, that "the Spirit intercedes for the saints" (i.e., for all Christians) and that this wordless communion is "according to God" (i.e., in accordance with his will and purpose). In other words, God discovers deep within our hearts exactly what we need most. Paul had just said that *we*, because of weakness, *cannot* pray as God would have it done (v. 26); but now he hastened to add that *the spirit,* who knows no weakness, *can* pray in just that fashion (v. 27). Only God truly knows his own mind and will, thus the true impulse for prayer must somehow flow *from* him *to* him, which is exactly what these verses depict by overcoming the tension between divine immanence and transcendence.

Does not this insight provide the most satisfying explanation of how God answers prayer? Looking back, we realize that we have prayed for a thousand foolish things. Even our best friends have asked amiss on our behalf. How can God make any sense of all these clumsy efforts to pray? Only by listening not to our faltering lips but to the intercessions of the Spirit, and answering only those entreaties that are "according to God." This is really what is signified by offering prayer "in Jesus' name," a plea that God will respond to that which breathes the spirit of his unique life and ignore that which echoes our ignorance and selfishness. No sensitive person could take prayer with ultimate seriousness unless it had this safeguard of the Spirit's guidance.

Here, then, is the grandest conception of prayer in all religious literature: *the God within us interceding to the God above us.*[7] Which means that, finally, prayer is grace and not a work of which we may boast. We do not pray alone in order to secure a divine help that is absent; rather, we pray at all only because we already have a divine help that is present. Prayer is not our meandering search for a missing God; rather, it is our participation in that eternal striving of Father, Son, and Spirit to restore creation's glory which catches us up, even without being aware of it, into the life of the Trinity itself. That is why we dare to believe that "by the power [of the Spirit] at work within us [God] is able to do far more abundantly *than all that we ask or think*" (Eph. 3:20 RSV).

NOTES

1. Ernst Käsemann, *Perspectives on Paul* (Philadelphia: Fortress Press, 1971), p. 131.
2. For details see William E. Hull, "Two Types of Thanksgiving" (Shreveport: First Baptist Church, Nov. 23, 1975), sermon #14.
3. That this is the force of the Greek phrase *katho dei* ("as we ought") is shown by the parallel phrase *kata theon* ("according to God") in v. 27. In other words, as an address to the Almighty, prayer must be on God's terms, which standard we cannot attain in our "weakness."
4. Tennyson, *In Memoriam.*

5. On the theme of prayer as a "cry," see John Knox, *Life in Christ Jesus* (Greenwich, Conn.: Seabury, 1961), pp. 105-8.
6. On the treatment of divine pathos in the prophets, see Abraham J. Heschel, *The Prophets* (New York: Harper, 1962), pp. 221-323.
7. C. H. Dodd, *The Epistle of Paul to the Romans* (London: Hodder and Stoughton, 1932), p. 136.

FESTO KIVENGERE

The Cross and World Evangelization

"Man," the upward-looking one, became a creature in dilemma when he lost his bearings (his compass direction). This tragic experience happened when the upward-looking one turned away from the direction of life and became the downward-looking one or the "inward-looking one." Away from the "life-direction" he turned to "death-direction." Away from light he turned to darkness. Away from the center he became eccentric. No wonder the inspired record described man in this state as "lost"!

Life fell apart—the world became *strange and hostile,* man's fellowman became *a threatening stranger.* Circumstances went out of his control. He lost the ability to cope with himself, his circumstances, and his neighbor. An uncomfortable awareness of emptiness—sometimes less felt, sometimes more acutely felt, but increasingly crippling—dogged his life.

His life has, since this experience commonly called the Fall, always been lived in the midst of conflicting pulls:

1) The upward pull toward the original ideal;
2) The downward pull toward deterioration into the base kind of living of slavery to violent appetites and passions;
3) The outward pull toward things and people against him;
4) The inward pull toward his own likes, feelings, and ambitions.

Taken from *Let the Earth Hear His Voice,* © 1975, World Wide Publications, Minneapolis, MN, U.S.A.

The cry of his heart seems always to have been, "Oh, for a balanced existence in the midst of these great pulls!" It is into these life-breaking contradictions that *God, in Christ,* came. For man in such conflicts was destroying himself. Therefore, God took up the rescue in his self-sacrificing love! "God was personally present in Christ, bringing this hostile world of men back into friendship with himself," says Paul (II Cor. 5:19). Thus as he was baptized in the River Jordan among sinners—sinless as he was—refusing to be counted apart from those he came to rescue, so God's good news, which is Jesus Christ, with outstretched arms in a mighty embrace, lay hold of our broken lives on *the cross* and its almighty act of love, condemned the hosility to death, releasing the captives.

So the Cross of Christ became God's almighty salvation for us sinners:

a) *In its divine origin*—ending our despair of ever reaching God through our futile man-made endeavors to goodness and providing the fresh and life-giving way to fellowship with God (Gal. 4:4, 5);

b) *In its downward reach*—getting beyond the very roots of our depravity and helplessness, thus dealing with our deepest need of moral dilapidation and releasing the cripples;

c) *In its inward penetration*—replacing our wrong center, which made us *self-centered*—by the new and right center—Christ, who makes us "Christ-centered" and so rescues *us from our inner fragmentation. The Cross brings inner wholeness.*

d) *In its outward outreach*—removing the conflicting elements in our relationship with our fellowmen as well as our world as a whole.

Here, then, is the centrality, the all-roundness, the cruciality of the Cross (the self-sacrificing love of God in Christ—in the sharing of God's good news with his world in evangelism).

Let us now look at the Cross in its practical aspect in evangelism:

1. *The Cross is the message of evangelism.* There is no

Christian faith without the Cross. Christianity was born *on the Cross.* It was the love on the Cross of Calvary that broke down all the barriers of *cultural, national, racial,* and *intellectual pride;* which stifled religious aspirations with their (anthropocentric) *humanistic* polarizations.

a) The Cross spells out the desperate moral need of man. Nothing less than the love that God demonstrated in Christ on the Cross could have come anywhere near to meeting our deep-seated *guilt.* And any so-called good news which does not reach this shuddering need of our moral insolvency is not worthy of the name. Nor is any evangelism which does not deal with his universal human malady worthy of the name. The Cross primarily deals with human moral guilt, and divine judgment over it, and his forgiveness. The Cross is, therefore, the message of *good news* to all men everywhere.

b) The Cross spells out how seriously God dealt with our sin. It is the price love paid to remove the tragic estrangement our sin had brought between us and God and between us and our fellow.

2. *The Cross is the motivating power of evangelism.* It is in the light shed from the Cross that scales fall from our eyes and we begin to see the wonder of his incredible redeeming love and the utter wretchedness of our sinfulness. In the Cross, for the first time, we see the reality of the wholeness of Jesus Christ for undone humanity, we see in this "whole Christ" on our behalf, for our well-being, as P. T. Forsyth puts it, "full judgment, indeed, there, but the grace uppermost, as he bears in himself his own judgment on us" (*Person and Place of Christ,* p. 74).

As the Holy Spirit illumines this great act of divine love "for us," the dawn of the glorious hope rises upon the whole human race with healing in its wings! In the rays of this redeeming love we see as never before that God has removed the once impenetrable barrier in our way of approach to him, and now he forgives us upon what he has borne for our sins on the Cross! Through the Cross we have free entry into an open presence of God! Thus the Cross becomes *the motivating power in evangelism*. All are welcome. There is no too-far-gone case in the light of this tremendous love! In the midst of *chaos, tumult,* and *philosophies of despair,* and sad divisions among professing Christians, we can lift our voices still, and point to the only place of healing—to the Cross. God was present in Christ, removing the polarizing barriers between us and him and bringing us into friendship with himself (and with one another).

3. *The Cross is the inspiration of evangelism.* The Cross is the flesh and bones, the heartbeat of evangelism; divert from this vital pulse and, inevitably, what remains of evangelism is a dry exercise in neatly put, but lifeless, statements of faith, devoid of power to heal broken lives and broken relationships. We may be as morally upright as the elder brother who never disobeyed a single order from his father and yet was completely out of tune with his father's attitude toward his returning brother! Here, I would like to pause and plead with you all as well as myself to reexamine our attitude toward our brothers and sisters whom we regard as being outside the pale of the evangelical camp. Are you in tune with the Father's attitude toward those outside your own conviction? Are we as uncompromising in love as we are in criticism of those "for whom Christ died," outside our own circle of conviction? Paul makes a penetrating statement under the inspiring power of the Cross in II Corinthians 5:21, "God (in his incredible love for us) treated Christ as sin, who knew no sin, for us sinners that we may be brought into right relationship with God through him." If this is what God went through to bring us into right relationship with himself, then we are left no room, no choice for any aloof attitude toward any of his children! There is no justification whatsoever for any other attitude than that of the love he demonstrated on Calvary's Cross for the world. Evangelism flowed direct from the Cross toward those who were in the very act of crucifying the Lord, to desperate criminals crucified with him! The Cross inspires evangelism and there is no other inspiration for evangelism besides.

4. *The Cross—the price of evangelism.* According to

biblical record, the good news became a living practical reality for us men when he who was equal with God "emptied himself" of all glory in order to come and share our humanness. It cost him his life to reach us in our misery. According to the prophet of evangelism, Isaiah: "He has poured out his soul unto death. . . . He was counted as a sinner among sinners." And as James Denney clearly puts it in his book, *The Death of Christ*, "The regenerating power of forgiveness depends upon its cost." The Cross spells out in shining letters that there was no limit to which God could not go in his redeeming love. The challenge that grips the whole life as one sees the extent of what God was willing to undergo on our behalf on Calvary, is so penetrating that all values are evaluated, the whole outlook is changed, and, most of all, what we regarded as sacrifice becomes humbling privilege. This is what filled Isaac Watts' heart with wonder and praise as he sang:

> Were the whole realm of nature mine,
> That were an offering far too small;
> Love so amazing, so divine,
> Demands my soul, my life, my all.

This is what Paul meant when in the light of impending danger to his life, he burst out, "But life is worth nothing unless I use it for doing the work of telling others the Good News about God's mighty kindness and love" (Acts 20:24).

Paul's words echo those of the Lord, who actually hung on the Cross, before he was crucified, "I have a terrible baptism ahead of me, and how I am pent up until it is accomplished" (Luke 12:50).

This is the only way we can look at our lives—our possessions, our gifts, our status and abilities—in the light of the Cross in evangelism. Any witness who evades this price is out of focus with the Cross, and falls short of the target of evangelism. We must reexamine our priorities in evangelism in the light of the Cross. May the Lord spare us the deadening tendency of resting in neat, evangelical clichés, of sheltering ourselves in secure fences round our lovely cliques, by the power of his liberating Cross. Then we, as his disciples, shall stand where the Master stood and then all we are and have will flow in gratitude to him, and in service to the world he died to save.

Can we still withhold anything in the light of the Cross, and still claim to follow him?

> Love so amazing, so divine,
> Demands my soul, my life, my all!

5. *The Cross is the uniting power of evangelism.* Only through the constraining vision of Christ and him crucified can the Christian church repent of its unfortunate weakening divisions and dividedness in its ranks, the wastage of its manpower, and the corroding hoarding of its material means. We need to catch a fresh vision of our Lord's words: "He who spares, loses" and "He who lets go, gains"; and the commentary of these words seems to me to come from Paul's words in Rom. 8:32, "He did not spare even his own Son, but instead of sparing him he gave him up on our behalf." This is the right attitude of those of us who have looked at the Cross, toward the material means available for us in this ministry. The Cross is where there can never be any justification for the *"hoarding attitude,"* the *"sparing attitude,"* the *"withholding attitude."* This sparing attitude does not apply to money and buildings only, but it covers persons as well. It is our physical lives which are to be offered as a living sacrifice to God. There is a tragic practice among those of us who desire to further the cause of evangelism to hoard gifts in our denominational ghettos, while open fields go on starving for good teaching and preaching. There are wealthy pockets of the Christian community who are unaware of needy areas where good men have no facilities for training for preaching the good news. May the Holy Spirit so inspire our spirits with the consuming vision of "he did not spare even his own Son," during this Congress, that we shall leave here under the compelling vision of God's love in Christ for the world as we see it *in the Cross.*

6. *The Cross is the drawing power of evangelism.* It is the Lord Jesus himself who drew the attention of his bewildered disciples at the end of his physical ministry—as it is recorded in John's Gospel (12:32): "When I am lifted up (on the cross) above the earth, I will draw all men to me." No matter what methods we may use in sharing the good news with men, still the drawing power is the Cross of Christ. It is Christ, the one crucified, who wins rebellious lives, melts stony hearts, brings life to the dead, and inspires stagnant lives into unsparing activity. It is the crucified who makes us see the world *alive with need for forgiveness.* It is the crucified who crosses out our fancies and introduces us to the inestimable value of people. It is the crucified Christ who destroys our prejudiced evaluations of our fellowmen as racial cases, tribal specimens, social outcasts or aristocrats, sinful characters, and religious misfits, by giving us the fresh evaluation of all men as redeemable persons on whose behalf Christ died. Evangelism fails miserably when its purpose becomes to draw men to its programs of preaching or social concern. Men are to be drawn by the power of the self-sacrificing love of God in Christ into new life in him. The Cross gives flesh and bones to evangelism. It is in the Cross that the truth becomes incarnate and reaches us where we are and as we are. It is the Cross which encourages us to cross over the barriers of our particular camps to meet God's world. The Cross of Christ is the panacea for the deep troubles of the human race. It is the hope for my beloved country of Africa with all its conflicting problems. It is the panacea for the so-called richer nations of the West, with their disturbing disintegrations of lives in the midst of material plenty.

Christ, the one crucified, is the power and the wisdom of God in evangelism. The Holy Spirit uses the Cross to remove not only sin and guilt, but also the crippling effects of fear and suspicion: the Cross is God's liberating power in evangelism.

We can never speak about the Cross and remain immune! The revelation through the Cross brings all sorts of men into the focus of the soul! It is under such exposure that you may have to leave your religious exercise (sacrifice) on the altar and go first and be reconciled to your brother; and then come and continue your worship!

The Cross in evangelism forces us to go and wash our Judah's feet in ministering love. In conclusion, I plead that as we receive the bread and the cup we will open our hearts to the estranged brothers and sisters. That we will allow the Cross to lead us out of the spiritual ghettos of our security—to him—and as we go out to him we shall meet many who come to him from other camps and shall have fellowship with them around the Cross. Then the communion with him and with one another will be a life-liberating and satisfying experience, sparking off the fire of evangelism for which our churches are in desperate need. And our age is waiting for the redemption of God's children from the corroding influences of this world's powers of evil into the glorious liberty of the fullness of life in the new kingdom of our Lord. Let us approach with boldness, and enter the presence of God through the Cross and enjoy fellowship with God and with one another, and by the power of the Holy Spirit proclaim God's good news to our age. "As for me—God forbid that I should boast about anything except the cross of our Lord Jesus Christ" (Gal. 6:14).

JAMES EARL MASSEY

Something of Value

Are not five sparrows sold for two pennies?
And not one of them is forgotten before God.
Why, even the hairs of your head are all numbered.
Fear not: you are of more value than many sparrows.
                                        —Luke 12:6-7 RSV

"You are of . . . value." There are times when we are
tempted not to believe this about ourselves, and sometimes
other people act as if they don't believe this about us either.
How often have you felt like nothing? Or, how often have
you dared to judge another man's worth? As a child
growing up in the city I heard many names and epithets
hurled in temper, things said to hurt and wound the hearer
and make him feel of no worth. I have seen the same thing
happen among adults who certainly knew better than to
act and speak that way. Not everybody will speak
injuriously to others. Some persons maintain enough
control to hold back certain thoughts, refusing to speak
them because they know how unkind such speech would
be. It is an old, old story: we know that a sense of personal
value is hard won, and it is not easily maintained in such a
world. So we all favor those who treat us with respect. We
all "like" those who by their treatment make us feel like a
treasured friend. And how we avoid those persons who
treat us otherwise! We recoil from anything that seems to
threaten our sense of worth, be it a person or an unwanted
experience. The text holds the word of Jesus to us, a word

reminding us of our value when circumstances seem to deny that we count at all.

I

Like sparrows, *we too feel so small* in such a big and threatening world. So many things militate to make us feel so small. For instance, we want to look ahead to the future, but looking ahead is not easy—events are proliferating in an entirely unpredictable fashion. So we are tempted to look back. But looking back is not safe, because pausing too long in a backward look can only put us behind. While some futurists complain that improvements among us are not occurring as fast as they could and should, not keeping pace with our abilities, others among us lament that change is too much with us, and they are tempted to look suspiciously at anything new.

Which of us above thirty has not questioned the system that now surrounds us, a system that boasts a "new math," a "new English," indeed a "new learning"? Perhaps you too recall the magazine cartoon picturing two college coeds coming down the campus library steps. With their arms loaded down with books, the one girl lamented to her friend, "Every day there are more and more things to be ignorant about!" Our kind of world does stir within us the feeling of being so small.

Certain kinds of living have played their sad part also. With parents scrambling to get ahead, children are sometimes neglected, overlooked, and mistreated. Again and again I have counseled adults who were still hurting from childhood wounds from parental neglect or mistreatment. Most of those persons needed a healthy sense of self; they also held antagonistic feeling for one of the parents.

While waiting in a shopping center for my wife to complete her shopping list, I browsed in the book department there. I chanced to overhear a young wife suggestively pleading with her husband: "Here is something you could give to your dad for Christmas." Her tone sounded so final, and weary, as if the couple had been searching now for some time. The husband drew near and examined the object she lifted to his view. Having heard her, I also turned, somewhat casually, and took a sidelong glance. The object was an excellently crafted model ship done in handcarved wood. The young man grabbed for the price tag, then acted stunned as he blurted out, "Ugh! thirty-five dollars!" Then with a scowl, he snapped, "But he's not worth *that much!*" I shuddered, wondering what had that father done to spoil the son's regard for him. I found myself wondering what price tag would have pleased him? How much is a father worth? How much is a son or a daughter worth? I finally concluded that that son had feelings against his father; he was hurting inside from something his father had or had not done toward him. Now, in his search for a cheap gift, he was betraying his own cheap view of his father's worth. That son did not feel valued, so he was unwilling to confer value. If only he had known his worth in the sight of God! If only that young man could have forgiven his father! If he could find release from his feelings, that husband could be an agent of love to make his father sense his worth. Our text is for that son, and ourselves. It is for all whom life has made feel so small—and even dared to act as less than we are. "You are of . . . value."

II

Like sparrows, *we too feel helpless* before the strong winds of life.

I looked out of our picture window one evening after an afternoon of storm winds in our city. Tree limbs were down here and there, and a few power lines were being repaired by city work crews. But I remember most the sight of a dead bird lying in the flower box beneath the window. The storm winds had been too strong for that bird to fight! Either that, or the clear plate glass had fooled the bird, appearing like a retreat into which it could fly for safety and rest. As I watched that scene of death I thought about our text.

There is stark realism in Matthew's parallel account of our text: "sparrows fall" (10:29)—but not without the noticing eye of God. Sparrows alight and feed, always under God's careful attention; but sparrows also fall, pushed or pulled by wind currents—or by some calculating child with a slingshot or rifle.

That word "fall" is a world of pictured circumstances. Like sparrows, men also fall, victims of life and living. This is the problem to which Jesus speaks. He reminds us that our worth is not diminished by tragedies, distresses, necessities. Men do fall: victims of hunger, poverty, wars, diseases, natural calamities, calculated cruelties. Men fall victim to the sins of other men—and their own!

All of us have known and felt that deep-seated concern to stay alive, and we have experienced that equally painful ache for the courage to live. The taste for life is so often frustrated by the terrors of life. A noted scientist of our time was writing about this problem when he explained: "on certain days the world seems a terrifying thing: huge, blind and brutal. It buffets us about, drags us along, kills us with complete indifference . . . sweep[s] away in one moment what we had laboriously built up and beautified with all our intelligence and all our heart."[1] Sparrows fall. Men fall, but our value is not diminished by the happening. Despite the experience, our value remains. "You are of . . . value."

III

Like sparrows, *we too seem so common* as to be of comparatively little worth. In Jesus' day, five sparrows could be bought for two pennies, and the more you bought the greater the discount. Volume decreased value, or so it seemed. But in God's sight it is not so.

Almost four billion persons people our world. Of what value can any one person be in the midst of so many? The New Testament word for "value" holds an insightful detail: it means to be differentiated, regarded as important because unique. It is true that humanity is of one common order, but there is a separateness and uniqueness of every person within that common order. This idea is well expressed by the saying, "God must have loved common people; he made so many of them." We might be stupified by the vast multitude around us in the world, and we might tend to miss the particularity of the persons we see in the mass, but God still deals with us individually, in "minute particulars," as William Blake explained it. Jesus was talking about the intimacy of God's dealings with us when he said, "The very hairs of your head are all numbered." "You are of . . . value."

IV

Jesus has spoken to us all. He knew that we humans wrestle with that painful uneasiness of mind called anxiety. Fully aware of our problem, that it is common to mankind, Jesus has spoken to reinforce our stand as we live in such a world. His words give us insight into God and ourselves. This text does not give us a systematic statement about life itself; it does not explain why life is as we find it, but it does give us a comforting and reassuring word about God and the help we are given as we live. Jesus has not tried to harmonize life as we know it with life as we wish it to be, but he has reminded us of our importance in the sight of God. Although we sometimes feel so little, so helpless, so common and undistinguished, that feeling is not the full or final fact about ourselves. We need not be ruined by emotional chaos caused by feelings of creaturehood. We are of value.

V

Dr. T. Franklin Miller tells of being on a ship at sea and having to miss his scheduled arrival time in Montreal because his ship went to the rescue of a man, deathly sick, on another ship about five hundred miles away. The ship bearing the sick man did not have a doctor or the surgical facilities needed if he was to live. There was nervous excitement aboard the passenger liner as that ship hurried toward the stricken man. At the time of rendezvous the sick man was transferred to the passenger vessel, and surgery was performed on him with successful results. The passenger liner docked at Montreal one day late, and nine hundred passengers were beset by complications with train, bus, and air travel connections: all because of *one man*—one man in need![2]

How did those passengers react to the forced change of plans? Dr. Miller talked with several of them during the hours of travel to reach the sick man. He was happily surprised that not one person with whom he talked had a single criticism about the rescue action. Personal inconveniences notwithstanding, every person seemed pleased that their ship could assist at such a time of need. That reaction was more than a mere matter of being nice about the inevitable delay. There was a real concern to help—because everybody knew that the sick man was a *person,* he had worth, he was someone, he had value.

Only God fully knows our value. He made us, so only he can fully measure our worth. But we get some understanding of how God values us when we look at what he has done in our interest through Jesus Christ. We are of such value in his sight that Jesus died for us, "the righteous [one] for [us] unrighteous, that he might bring us to God" (I Pet. 3:18). Only when we live in God's will is our worth focused, realized, and fulfilled.

NOTES

1. See Pierre Teilhard de Chardin, *The Divine Milieu* (New York: Harper, 1960), p. 117; see also Christopher F. Mooney, *Teilhard de Chardin and the Mystery of Christ* (New York: Harper, 1966), esp. pp. 13-33.
2. See his editorial, "Rendezvous in the North Atlantic," *Christian Leadership* magazine, Oct. 1959, pp. 3, 20.

JÜRGEN MOLTMANN

Liberation
Through Reconciliation

*That is, in Christ God was reconciling the world to
himself, not counting their trespasses against
them, and entrusting to us the message of
reconciliation. So we are ambassadors for Christ,
God making his appeal through us. We beseech
you on behalf of Christ, be reconciled to God.*
—II Corinthians 5:19-20 RSV

*Therefore, if any one is in Christ, he is a new
creation; the old has passed away, behold, the new
has come.*
—II Corinthians 5:17 RSV

With these unforgettable words, the Apostle Paul brings
together the sum of the Christian message from God, the
basis of faith and the practice of new life.

This is God, who in Jesus Christ takes the path to the
cross, who takes suffering upon himself in order to
reconcile the world. He dies the death of deepest
forsakenness in order to give his love to the world. He
becomes poor in order to make many rich.

That is the world in which we live, suffer, and
struggle—the creation which is not cast off, which is

This message was presented by Dr. Moltmann to the General Assembly
of the Reformed World Confederation in Nairobi, 1970. From *The Gospel
of Liberation* by Jürgen Moltmann, translated by H. Wayne Pipkin,
copyright © 1973 by Word, Inc. Used by permission of Word Books,
Publisher, Waco, Texas 76703, and the author.

reconciled, loved, and not forsaken by God in the cross of Christ. It is not accused, but acquitted. It shall live and not perish.

And thus are we—in communion with Christ, a new creation free from the law of the old, perishing world, free from anxiety before its lords and powers, free from sin and death, and now open for the new life in joy, open for the salvation of the entire waiting creation, open for the coming creative affairs of God.

"Look, everything has become new. Look to the dying Christ and you see the dawn of the coming day of God who will transform everything!"

That is our lesson—to invite all men to the place of the poor, suffering, and dying Christ for reconciliation with God, to their new future, to freedom, to peace, and to righteousness. His cross is the symbol of hope for this earth. The reconciliation of God is the eternal living source of liberation for guilt-laden and dying men, for the degraded and wronged, for the poor and suffering.

Whoever believes in the God of reconciliation begins to suffer in this unredeemed world. He can no longer put up with the circumstances in the separated churches in the divided world, and the inhuman society. He has become different. The world must not remain as it is. It is open for its freedom—its redemption—because it is reconciled in Christ. We hope for the future transformation of the world because we believe in the reconciliation of God.

Whoever believes in reconciliation begins to suffer in the church. The word *reconciliation* has been misused and betrayed by historical Christendom itself. False prophets speak of peace and call to peace where there is no peace. They comfort the people in their misfortune, telling them it is not at all so bad (Jer. 8:11). Appeasement is substituted for reconciliation, and religion is misused for the purpose of keeping the poor quiet so that the sufferers will be satisfied with unrighteousness and not protest it strongly. Faith is thus made to inhibit desire and deaden emotional states. The striving parties are called to reconciliation, to stay neutral and not take up sides. When we long for reconciliation with our enemies to whom we do wrong, we avoid therewith the confession of our own guilt. We exchange love with toleration over against evil.

Can one believe the churches, which preach reconciliation to others but do not themselves practice it so concretely as Jesus did when he healed the sick, cast out demons, and sat at the table with sinners and tax collectors? Why do many Christians turn away from the church and finally join social-revolutionary movements or new messianic cults? They see the churches and parishes to be more reconciled with the privileged of society and the good opinion of the powerful than with the crucified one. For this reason, the rebels hate the word of reconciliation, for they see everywhere the untruthful practice of "appeasement," which does not live and act "in the place of Christ," but is concerned for one's own salvation.

Reconciliation means new community with God and one another. How shall this new community be testified to credibly by the divided church? The separation of Christendom into various churches, their grudging concurrence in missions, the mutual discrimination of Christians through the laws of different churches is a scandal. It is a scandal not only before the world which sees this sad drama, but much more still a shameful scandal before the sorrow of the dying Christ.

If the churches of society today want to give something of Christendom, that is, of reconciliation, then they must let themselves be renewed. Whoever believes is in the first place Christ's, and only in the second place a member of "his" church. His suffering in "his" church springs out of his love for Christ who has loved him together with the world. Does this love for Christ and for the world lead forth today from among the established churches?

In many churches today, we find, to be sure, youth movements not only for a social-revolutionary transformation of the world, but also for the sake of Christ. These youth no longer find Christ in the church; they find him in the slums.

The church which has been separated for centuries finds

itself today on the way—as we hope—to an ecumenical community. Modern social-revolutionary criticism of the churches, whether they are now separated or united, places us before new fronts in Christendom such as we have never before known but will be becoming ever more familiar with in the future.

In this situation, we should not shun suffering in the church in the love of Christ for the world, either through a conservative flight backward or a modernistic flight forward. Accepting that suffering, we may productively ask from it a new, credible community of Christ. Then, through God's reconciliation, can the churches be free again from their neglect and their downfall to the powers of this world. That is our hope for the church of Christ. We believe in the one church of God, liberated through reconciliation.

Whoever believes in reconciliation begins to suffer for the divided world. We have had to bury many hopes which were set on the humanization of the world by science, technology, rational business, and world politics. We live in a divided and alienated world. One division follows upon another, while, in a paradoxical way, the world grows ever more together into "one world." The Second World War left behind the East-West conflict, leading to the earth's division into the spheres of influence of the two white superpowers—Russia and America. Over the last twenty years the economic conflict between the rich peoples of the north and the poor peoples of the southern hemisphere has increasingly entered into the foreground. To the ideological conflict between capitalism and socialism has been added the race conflict. Wherever today are found race conflicts, ideological differences, social, religious, and national tensions, political peace will not be brought about through reconciliation; rather, there will be division, expulsion, dissension, apartheid, and ghettos. In Berlin an ideological wall was built. In Belfast there is a religious barbed wire fence. In South Africa and North America the making of ghettos continues. Whole populations in the Near East, in India, in Indochina have been expulsed and persecuted so that the different are among themselves. Divided cities, divided countries, separated men, castes and class systems mark the face of this earth on which men apparently can and want to live in a nonhuman way with other men. The motto of all conquerors who disseminate unfreedom is "divide and conquer," "rule through division." The life of mankind is oppressed by division and lordship. In this divided world, appeasement is no means of reconciliation, only a means to survive while one separates the strugglers and postpones their mutual annihilation.

Whoever believes in reconciliation begins to suffer at the inhumanity of man and his society. Wherever man leaves his humanity and makes for himself proud and doubtful gods of himself and his neighbors, he is inhuman, he has anxiety before himself and his neighbors. He can no longer love. And, loving only himself, he misuses his experiences, his possessions, and his neighbors for his own self-righteousness. They all must constantly say to him who he actually is and must appease his inner uncertainty. In his anxiety he depends on transitory things that must support his self-confidence. He expects from the good things of creation what only the creator himself can give him. He changes the splendor of the invisible God into an image just like transitory man (Rom. 1:23). He changes the truth of God into a lie and serves creation more than the creator (Rom. 1:25).

"The heart of man is an idol factory," said Calvin correctly. That shows up ahead of everything in the religion of man, which is always a "religion of anxiety." In this sense, man is indestructibly religious. His world is full of idols, gods, fetishes, and person cults—even his modern world. However, if man's heart depends on such idolized values and realities, then he is no longer free to accept the reality of his life without illusion and resignation, nor the different life style of anyone else. Every attack on his idols becomes an attack on his better self, and he reacts to it with murderous aggression. As such an idolater, man is in fact a neurotic being. Human societies which through political religions have lifted idolatry to the level of a cult are inhuman. Men are brought to sacrifice to the moloch of one's own proud nation. Humanity is brought to sacrifice to the fetishism of goods and consumption. While man has anxiety for the loss of his own pride, he is not ready for peace. The idol factory runs full course in our nations.

Christ or these idols—that is the question. Whoever experiences liberation from anxiety by faith in the Crucified begins to suffer in the inhuman pressure of this anxiety. Whoever follows after the person who is crucified by the idols and powers of this world becomes ready also to be an iconoclast of freedom against those gods and cults of his society.

To demonstrate and to practice human liberation through God's reconciliation in this time means to preserve the long breath of hope between hate and rage, between reaction and revolution. We should consciously accept the sorrow of this time, making the cry for freedom out of the depth of the oppressed nations and men to be our own sighs and groans and answering with a call to reconciliation. The world can be made free through reconciliation. That is our hope for divided humanity—a humanity tormented by the idols of its anxiety. We believe in the one new humanity of God which is liberated through reconciliation.

Yet what is reconciliation? How does God reconcile in such a way that our ideals and our anxious dreams are broken and our divided and enslaved world changes and becomes free? Where is the reconciling God at work?

Whichever way Christian faith and theology today would like to go, Christ alone is our reconciler and our liberator. Whoever wants to know what reconciliation actually is must look to the path of Jesus. Jesus made the reconciliation of God real with the godless by healing the sick, driving out demons, fraternizing with lepers, sinners, and tax collectors, by championing the poor and oppressed. He lived and knew God's reconciliation in the midst of the conflicts of his divided society. The way of the Crucified became the way to the cross. In the loneliness of his death, the reconciliation and the liberation of the entire godless world took place through the love of the Father.

What differentiates Christian faith from other religions and revolutions is the lordship of the Crucified. His cross separates faith from unfaith just as much as from superstition. What Christians believe and do must always be manifest and made righteous before the face of the Crucified. For through his suffering and death God once for all reconciled the forsaken world with himself, accepted it, and disclosed its freedom. Jesus did not reconcile God, but God himself reconciled the world with himself through the death of Jesus.

The cross of Christ makes public the cost of reconciliation (John 3:16).

The resurrection of the Crucified opens the universal future to the freedom it originated.

Let us make the cost of reconciliation clear. God did not liberate Israel out of slavery in Egypt through reconciliation with the pharaoh, but by the rescue of the persecuted and the defeat of the persecutor at the Red Sea (Exod. 14). According to Isaiah's vision of the future, for the salvation of his people out of the Babylonian exile this God will bring a great and distant people to sacrifice (Isa. 43:1-7). According to the gospel of the "new covenant," however, in the suffering and the death of Christ God brings his own son, that is, God himself, to sacrifice in love for the freedom of the world. In other words, the destruction and judgment have become so great, so world-wide, that God himself gets up and bears the sins of the world. Forsaken by God and men, Jesus dies lonely on the cross, thus taking on himself the loneliness and forsakenness and the burden of destruction for the entire world. That act creates freedom, peace, and a new joy for this world and all men in their life. This reconciliation is not simply maintained. It is no law.

This reconciliation comes into being through the representative suffering of Christ and the sacrifice of love. God did not look after himself, but gave himself for the reconciliation of the world and its freedom.

Reconciliation is an expensive grace. While God took the corruptions of the world on himself, he created for the world its new future in redemption. We must understand that in the very suffering and death of Christ, God creates something new. God is "for us," for us sinners. God is "with us," with us godless ones. Reconciliation with God is created only by God himself. He is the subject and we are the objects of reconciliation. Therefore, the representation of Christ also is exclusive, unique, and unrepeatable. The reconciliation of God is the basis and the power for reconciliation between men who are enemies. God is "for us"; therefore, we can and should be "with one another" and not against one another.

The word from the cross is the gospel of God, as Paul says. Whover does not begin here to believe God, to live with him and to thank him has not yet begun with Christendom. We call the uncertainly developing Christianity to God in that we call all to the cross of Christ.

Reconciliation means here, in fact, that guilt is forgiven. We know very well that no man and no people can recognize and confess their own guilt because they would then lose all self-respect. Guilt, therefore, is mostly pushed aside. But guilt which is pushed aside works further and poisons the life of a man and an entire people with hate for others and anxiety for oneself. In the cross of Christ, however, the guilty are not called to account and penalized. They are drawn to love and liberated. Guilt must no longer be pushed aside, but can be accepted as guilt forgiven.

Reconciliation does not mean only the forgiveness of guilt, however, but also the liberation from the power of sin. For Paul, sin is not only a guilt which we have, but still more, a power which totally enslaves us. It is the godless bond of death which through anxiety wins power over men. Because of this anxiety, the inhuman in us makes idols in the hope of finding certainty in transitory things. Fertility becomes the idol of anxiety. The nation or a leader becomes the god of anxiety. Men who are different become the phantoms and the apparitions of anxiety.

Anyone who is anxious is controllable and can be extorted and exploited. Liberation from the power of sin is also, therefore, always liberation from anxiety, liberation from idols, liberation from hate for men who are different from ourselves. This liberation from the power of sin takes place through the power of reconciliation. We find it in the resurrection of the crucified Christ from the dead. In Romans 11:15 Paul has brought together these two ideas—the "reconciliation of the world" and "life out of death"—for in fact, in the resurrection of the Crucified for us the power of death has been taken. Whoever is grasped by the spirit of the resurrected, which is the spirit of freedom, has no more anxiety; he is the friend of God even though the world is at enmity with him. He laughs at the lords and powers of this world. The evil bond of his lordship is broken wherever the Crucified becomes the leader of life in freedom. Whoever has no fear is not governable. He can, to be sure, be shot dead; but "it is a wonderful thing if one suddenly has no more fear."

Where has this liberation through reconciliation happened? The proclamation of the reconciliation of God brought Jesus into a deadly conflict with the public powers of his time—with priests and politicians. He was expelled from their camp and died "outside the door" (Heb. 13:12) between other rejected ones. Reconciliation, then, is created not in a holy place, nor in a religious sphere, but in the midst of the world and, to be sure, in its deepest point at a shameful place for the lost. We should, therefore, not make a cult out of reconciliation, which, separated from the sorrow of the world, is celebrated in the stillness of the churches, but seek and receive the reconciliation of Christ there where he has suffered. "Let us go out, out of the camp and bear his humiliation," says Hebrews (13:13). Reconciliation is not a religious cult for the pious, but the justification of the godless and the love of God for his enemies in the midst of their world. We must not let liberation through reconciliation be cooped up in a religious ghetto. The power of resurrection wants to renew the entire world from the ground up.

If the cross of Christ did not stand in a holy place, but there "outside," then neither does reconciliation belong in the inner parts of personal piety of the heart. We cannot lock up reconciliation in the ghetto of our hearts. We must receive the reconciliation of Christ and his freedom of resurrection where he has suffered, and that means in the midst of the actual inhumanities of our society.

To whom is the reconciliation of God in Christ of value? Paul knows two horizons here: reconciliation is of value on one for us (II Cor. 5:18) and on the other for the world (II Cor. 5:19; Rom. 11:15; Col. 1:20; Eph. 2:16). These are not contradictions, for reconciliation is valid for us together with the entire enslaved creation and is intended for the world throughout our lives. The horizon of reconciliation is in fact not any more narrow than the breadth of the entire creation of God. His reconciliation reaches as far as the clouds go. If Christians keep reconciliation a secret for themselves and give to the rest of the world only their sympathy or their developmental help, they betray the cross. That is a "Christian caste" which shuts itself off from the rest of population. If all cannot be reconciled, we also are not actually reconciled. We should, therefore, break out of our churches and out of the anxious egoism of our nations and develop a new piety of solidarity with all the damned of this earth. "God was in Christ reconciling the world," and the churches are not yet already "the world," but in the best sense a small beginning of that reconciled world of God. Out of the tension between "us" as reconciled, and the "world" as reconciled by God, originates the mission of freedom, the engagement for peace, and the sortie for righteousness in the world. The floor burns under our feet when we recognize this tension.

Finally, we should not forget that the reconciliation of the world is created through the bodily death and resurrection of Christ. The salvation of the world is therefore not only the salvation of souls, but together with that, the salvation of the body. "The body belongs to the Lord and the Lord to the body," says Paul (I Cor. 6:13). He does not speak of a precedence of the soul. After having sounded the salvation of the soul and the rescuing of individuals for so long, we Christians are today beginning to discover the materialistic bodily components of salvation which lie in the new creation. "All the ways of God end in corporeality" (Otinger). Man is subjected bodily to death, sicknesses, hunger, exploitation, and degradation by other men. Together with the entire waiting creation Christians long bodily for salvation from transitoriness (Rom. 8:23). The reconciliation of the world completed in Christ opens to this world the wide and encompassing horizon of salvation, or redemption, of the kingdom in which God dwells with man. Salvation in this encompassing sense means Shalom—a new creation of the whole man according to the body and the soul, a new creation of the whole humanity according to persons and relationships, a new creation of Heaven and earth, so that righteousness and peace finally join together on earth. This is called resurrection. The more earnestly we take the bodily suffering and death of Christ, the more all-encompassing will we understand the eschatological horizon of freedom to be which his resurrection opens.

How is the reconciliation of the world with God exhibited in the symbol of the cross? How can we correspond to it credibly in word and deed? We accept here what the Reformed World Assembly thought and said in its last conference in Frankfurt under the theme "Come Creator Spirit."

The reconciliation in the cross is preached, lived, and accomplished in this unredeemed world through the power of the spirit. It is attested to by sermon, by community, and by deeds of righteousness. I would like to point out that the cross of Christ is not only the affair of Christian witnesses, but also impresses its form on this world.

Because we do not venture to state loudly and clearly enough that judgment which is bound with Christ by the cross, the word of reconciliation has indeed become cheap and unreal. The "word of reconciliation," however, is for Paul the "word from the cross"; this cross, which is for some a power of God, for many, however, is nothing other than folly and scandal (I Cor. 1:18).

Reconciliation really has nothing to do with an indifferent neutrality. Jesus Christ himself preached the gospel of the near kingdom of God to "the poor" and not to "the rich." He was a friend of sinners and lepers, and not of Pharisees. His mission was available to all men in that he became an intense partisan of the weak, the discriminated against, and the hopeless. Jesus grasped the entire human society, so to speak, at its lowest point with the despised ones. Throughout the Old Testament, in spite of the special covenant with the people Israel, there already occurs the deep recognition: you are a God of the needy, the refuge of the oppressed, the sustainer of the weak, the refuge of the forsaken, the savior of the doubting. Thus present and conducting himself, God "pushes the powerful from their thrones and lifts the lowly. He fills the hungry with good things and lets the rich go empty" (Luke 1:51-53). Just as all flesh should see "together" the splendor of the Lord, God lowers the mountains and raises the valleys.

If we grasp this partiality of God and of the gospel today, then we will also understand again the "revolutionary" character of the Bible. Only for the poor is the message a joyous message. For the rich and self-righteous, it is painful. The message of reconciliation is not the religious honesty of the good society, but the salt of the earth. And salt in the wounds of the earth burns, but it hinders decay. We must obtain again the sharpness of the gospel if we want to spread the freedom of the Crucified out into this chaotic world. "Woe be to us if we do not preach the gospel"—woe be to us if we do not preach the gospel, but the law.

In return "we are invited to the place of Christ," says Paul. The Crucified invites us through humanity to reconciliation with God. One who invites has no great power. His hands are open and extended invitingly. He forces no one and compels no man. His invitation grants freedom and time to the invited. His perseverance in offering always opens anew to them a reconciling and free future. Lords command, judges judge, party leaders proclaim. God, however, lets us be implored by the dying Christ. He is the liberating God in a world of slavery and rebellion.

Reconciliation is lived in Christian community. That is the second thing. But how does the cross show itself in the life of the reconciled? Human societies adapt themselves naturally in the likeness of their members. "Birds of a feather flock together," said Aristotle. The same class, the same race, the same nation, the same economic order, the same views, and the same morals unite us with men who are like us, who affirm us. Men who are different unsettle us. We naturally love friends and despise enemies. The law of life of a Christian community, however, is not just this homogeneity, but the "acceptance of the other" in his differentness. This acceptance and love joins the unlike. Christian community brings into focus the reconciliation of the enemy with God in a divided world then if it consists of "Jews and heathens, Greeks and barbarians, lords and slaves, men and women" (Gal. 3:28). The walls and fences of the ghettos which men erect against one another in order to maintain their own dignity are overturned and broken down by Christian community, for in the spirit of reconciliation, the Crucified himself steps between enemies and calls a new community into life (Eph. 2:14ff.). Old enemies and also old friendships break down in the face of the new creation in Christ. Then the church actually becomes the reconciling body of Christ.

But our churches and parishes are not like this. The natural and thus so inhuman principle of sociability always seems to succeed so that only the like find themselves together and the different ones remain outside the door. National churches, racial churches, class churches, middle-class churches, are in their practical life heathenish and heretical. Through them, not reconciliation but contempt is disseminated. Not until a Christian community consists of the unlike, of the educated and uneducated, of black and white, of the high and the low, will it come to be a witness of hope for the reconciled world of God. Such a community will have difficulty in the divided world. Its members will be considered traitors of the "most holy goods" of the respective society and class.

They will be a community under the cross. But we wait for such a community, for only in it lies hope.

The service of reconciliation takes place, finally, in actual deeds of liberation. The reconciliation in the cross of Christ has in itself a world-changing impulse. The Resurrection shows it to us. If the power of death is broken, then the power of fate is broken also. When the spirit of Resurrection rules, there is freedom—world-conquering freedom, and therefore also world-changing freedom. When, by virtue of reconciliation, guilt is forgiven and hostility is conquered, a new future opens for which it is worth living. Whoever is reconciled is also changed. If God has reconciled the world with himself, then all relationships in this world are changeable for the person who believes. Nothing must remain as it is. Everything can become new.

Reconciliation without a change of men and their relationships is a weak consolation. Christians should perceive that today. Change without reconciliation leads to terrorism. Revolutionaries should recognize that today. For not until there is reconciliation will the compulsion of the evil deed which bears continuous evil be broken. Not until there is reconciliation will the devilish circle of revenge be destroyed. Not until there is reconciliation will the law of retaliation be conquered. Creative new righteousness, creative peace, and a freedom such as the world has not yet scarcely seen originates out of reconciliation and not out of law.

The scheme of the divided world has eaten very deeply into human thought and feeling. It is our own anxiety which has taught us to hate the opponent. The person who preaches hate always has anxiety. It is through the propaganda of the dominant that the notion of friend-enemy dichotomy is brought to us. But Christ is not against the "Communists"; he died for them. Christ is not against the "whites"; he died for them. That demands from us a new thinking and a new solidarity of love, for only love overturns anxiety. Love includes the opponent in its thoughts and affairs. It sees in him the reconciled and liberated friend of tomorrow. It does now what is possible tomorrow, for it sees the opponent in the hands of the dying Christ. Love has, therefore, a critical trust in the changeability of the enemy and a permanent mistrust against the justice of one's own position.

In social and political conflicts, Christians are "unreliable confederates" for both sides. They also fight against unjust lords, against racists, and against exploiters. But they are immune to the leading of hate and of terror. They do not let the law of fighting be prescribed by the enemy, but with their own methods fight the battle to free opponents of conflict from their hate-producing and power-wielding anxiety. They know that God's reconciliation surrounds the opponent also, and therefore that righteousness can only be reached by mutual transformation. They cannot be forced to enter into the devilish circle of power and counterpower, for they want to overthrow this demonic circle and not to support it.

Mao says: "We intend, therefore, that war be abolished. We want no war. One can, however, only abolish war through war; and if one wants no more guns, one must take arms in hand" (*Words,* Peking 1967, p. 76). His enemies are exactly of the same persuasion. However, that is no hopeful dialectic, but a very doubtful one indeed. We intend, instead, that war be done away with. We too want no war. War can, however, only be done away with through creative peace. If we want arms no longer to be in hand, then we must fight for peace with the means of peace and make plowshares out of swords.

To be sure, it can be that Christians also doubt the removal of scientific and political unrighteousness with peaceful means and accept the recourse to power as the last resort. But they cannot justify the use of power, for then they assume guilt which must be forgiven. However, the person who does nothing in order not to be guilty still carries the responsibility of obedience to God. Mostly, however, we do not stop to consider this last question. Mostly, men are called to weapons because nothing better occurs to them in their anxiety. The person on whom this anxiety is no longer imposed should develop productive dreams for peace. We have invested rich scientific, technical, and strategic dreams in military death, but in life, in peace, powerless resistance, and the change of the opponent, on the other hand, almost no dreams.

Men who fight against each other, who persecute and destroy others, are reconciled in Christ even though they still are not redeemed. Thanks be to God. We and our enemies can be changed. The world itself has become a changeable world. God has made the impossible appear to be possible. Let us therefore already do today what shall be tomorrow. "The night is past, the day is coming near, let us finally do what we should" (Rom. 13:12), and grasp the freedom which reconciliation gives us.

JEAN MYERS

Naked, but Not Ashamed

Genesis 2:25

Throughout recorded history, men and women have displayed an insatiable desire, both in thought and deed, to return to Eden or Paradise before the Fall in an effort to "get it right this time"! Religious history and secular history contain countless attempts worldwide to reestablish a paradise including a reunion with God and fellowman. These attempts demonstrate a deep desire within mankind to strip away traditional and cultural restrictions for a return to a simple close communion between Creator and creation and to a unity in creation itself. Even the present-day American culture is not exempt. The recent film *Logan's Run* deals with this theme. Set in the future, the story revolves around a young man and a young woman who, when forced to flee for their lives or be destroyed, break forth from the dome under which their entire society was housed and begin anew on the outside—a new Adam and a new Eve.

As Christians, we usually regard these attempts to begin anew as futile. We say that there is no way to return to the life found in Eden, and we plod along accepting the burden of the sin of Adam and Eve. We acknowledge that we have forever lost the innocence which allowed Adam and Eve to stand naked before the Lord and before each other and feel no shame. We lament our estrangement from God and from one another and regret the layers of

Used by permission of Jean Myers.

burdensome clothes that have been placed upon us in the form of societal roles—and leave it at that. But, should we? John Milton, the seventeenth-century poet, answered this question for us in the opening lines of his famous poem *Paradise Lost,* as he wrote:

> Of Man's first disobedience, and the fruit
> Of that forbidden tree whose mortal taste
> Brought death into the world, and all our woe,
> With loss of Eden, till one greater Man,
> Restore us . . .

The key is found in this phrase—"till one greater Man Restore us": Christ! Milton realized, and so should we, that Christ restored man's relationship to God, stripping him of the vestments of estrangement and returning him to the Garden's close communion with God as a *new creature.* But that is not all! If we believe that Christ restored mankind to God, then we must also believe that Christ restored the original communication between fellow creatures—man to woman as person to person, without regard for sexual distinction or any other distinction imposed by society. Once again, through Christ, men and women could stand naked before God and each other and not be ashamed. What a liberating thought! Each one of us, male or female, has the inner desire to be accepted for who we are. The president of our seminary, Dr. McCall, put it this way in a recent article in the *Courier-Journal.* He stated that "I don't want to get an image of 'This is what a seminary president is, now act like a seminary president.' I want to say, 'I'm a human being. I'm a person. And just accept me as that'" (September 16, 1979).

Ministers today need to realize how lopsided the Christian message has been. Churches have recognized what Christ did for man's relationship to God, while at the same time, neglecting to see what Christ did to resolve the estrangement society has brought between men and women through traditional roles. This is dangerous! As women begin to realize their potential in secular society, the church should and must support women as they try to strip away the vestments of bondage placed on them by their traditional roles. If not, while men and women of God will not be estranged from God, they will become more estranged from each other. Churches will divide, families will divide, women called of God to be ministers will become discouraged and bitter, but worst of all, the gospel of Jesus Christ will be weakened. What a travesty not to bear witness to the message that "there is neither Jew nor Greek, there is neither bond nor free, there is neither male nor female: for ye are all one in Christ Jesus" (Gal. 3:28 KJV).

If, however, Christian ministers today *do* accept the challenge to restore the Genesis relationship of man to woman as it applies to women in the ministry, the message of Christ will be strengthened as the male and female counterparts of humanity both proclaim *together* the unity to be found with God and each other in Christ. Man and woman, through Christ, will be able to stand *together* before God, naked and not ashamed. What a beautiful idea—a vision of men and women in unison declaring God's love through Christ! How much better than competition and strife! How much more as God had intended!

A reestablished intimate communication between the male and female counterparts of God's creation—how do we get there? First, it is essential to keep in mind the example of Jesus. Evelyn and Frank Stagg adeptly reach the heart of Christ's attitude toward women when they write in their book, *Woman in the World of Jesus,* that "Jesus affirmed personhood, giving it its worth apart from sexuality or other distinctions" and in so doing, "according woman with the dignity, freedom and responsibility of a human being."[1]

Jesus accomplished the task of affirming personhood and granting woman with dignity, freedom, and responsibility in three particular ways as described by the Staggs. First, he was found "repeatedly on the side of the disadvantaged," desiring to bring them freedom from any physical or spiritual bondage. This group included woman. Jesus freed many women from physical bondage as he healed the woman bent double, the woman with the issue of blood, the daughter of the Syrophoenician woman, Jairus' daughter, and the son of the widow of Nain. Jesus also freed the woman caught in adultery and the Samaritan woman from the bondage of their sins.

Second, Jesus "freely socialized with women, without a hint that he feared for his reputation."[2] Rather, Jesus sought in his teachings about and relationships with women to elevate their position in society bringing them dignity. Three of Jesus' teachings in particular demonstrate his desire to elevate the position of woman in society. In his teaching concerning adultery, Jesus declared that adultery could be committed against a woman, even one with no husband. This was a new idea. Until this point, it was customary to believe that adultery could only be committed against a woman's husband. Here Jesus recognized the personal worth of woman. Also, Jesus taught that adultery could be committed in the heart as well as overtly, again elevating woman above the status of sex object. In Jesus' teachings concerning divorce, he championed the rights of the faithful wife not to be divorced, and gave the wife the same rights to divorce as her husband. Both of these ideas were in conflict with the Jewish customs of the day, which only allowed the woman to sue, asking a court to compel her husband to give her a divorce. In Jesus' teachings on remarriage, in Matthew, he "allowed divorce and remarriage to the innocent party where the spouse had been unfaithful,"[3] regardless of sex. In Jesus' relationships, again and again, he demonstrated his desire to bring dignity to woman. This is illustrated in his praise of the widow who offered the two mites and the two women who anointed him. It is also evident in his allowing women to accompany the Twelve and himself on evangelistic journeys and to minister with him. Jesus also recognized the conflict between the study and the kitchen in Mary and Martha and declared them both equally fit for woman.

Third, Jesus "honored women with a primary role in proclaiming his resurrection from the dead."[4] It is apparent that, as recorded in the four Gospels, "the risen Lord did choose to appear first to women (or a woman) and commission them (or her) to proclaim this most important fact to the disciples."[5] In this way, Jesus gave women the same responsibility of proclamation as he did his disciples, as he favored them with his risen presence first.

Now that we have in mind how Christ went about reestablishing the dignity, freedom, and responsibility of woman as a human being, it is imperative that we use Christ's example to help us develop some concrete ways of achieving the same end. Three particular concrete actions present themselves readily to be taken by the Christian minister. First, reject the subordination of women which has prevailed in the Southern Baptist denomination. Look at Christianity as seen through the life and teachings of Christ and this passage, and not as filtered through a few of the teachings of Paul or a misrepresentation of this creation account. Free women ministers from the Domestic Code and acknowledge Paul's own words, written earlier in Galatians 3:28, that "there is neither Jew nor Greek, there is neither bond nor free, there is neither male nor female: for ye are all one in Christ Jesus."

Second, elevate woman to an equal standing with man in the study of God's Word. Use the example of Mary, who was at least one of Christ's students in theology,[6] to lead those with whom you come in contact to accept and encourage women who choose to study theology rather than to pursue the traditionally accepted courses for women. Also, encourage your female colleagues day by day, for they need your support desperately.

And third, encourage women of God to share equally with men in the responsibility of the proclamation of God's Word. In so doing, you will not only be aiding women in achieving their highest potential, but you will also be lessening your own burden! Men and women will then stand before God, equally responsible for the proclamation of his Word. Also, men and women will stand before one another sharing one another's burdens and growing together in a more complete ministry. A good idea, don't you think?

Well—it's up to you now. You have seen through the ministry of Christ how it is possible once more to achieve the intended relationship of God to humanity and man to woman described in Genesis 2:25. Now you, through Christ, as ministers of the gospel, have the power to grant to the Christian community of Southern Baptists that which so many have longed for—the chance to "get it right this time." Please allow us, as women ministers, to walk with *God and you* once more in the Garden—a new Adam and a new Eve, naked, but not ashamed.

NOTES

1. Stagg and Stagg, *Woman in the World of Jesus* (Philadelphia: Westminster Press, 1978), pp. 111, 255.
2. *Ibid.*, p. 255.
3. *Ibid.*, p. 133.
4. *Ibid.*, p. 255.
5. *Ibid.*, p. 150.
6. *Ibid.*, p. 118.

DAVIE NAPIER

The Burning in the Temple

Introduction to Isaiah 6

The call of Isaiah took place twenty-seven centuries ago. That prophet had an exceptionally long life and ministry, extending over the reigns of at least four kings of his country, Judah. Isaiah was an urbanite, living in what was for him and his countrymen *the* city, Jerusalem. His language, his politics, and even his theology are impressively shaped by his urban existence.

And he is a man highly placed in Jerusalem, either by virtue of professional status or possibly by royal birth or by both. King Ahaz listens to him, if he does not heed him; and King Hezekiah, by any standard one of Judah's most distinguished kings, not only listens and heeds, but is strongly dependent on Isaiah.

I suppose we would have to say that none of the great Old Testament prophets is typical. Each is so powerfully himself. But no prophet represents classical prophetism more forcefully, more comprehensively, more eloquently, than Isaiah. He is, in the best sense of the word, the most sophisticated of the prophets. But it is finally his own honest, unneurotic, thoroughly realistic appraisal of himself and his own generation together with his historical and existential knowledge of the Word of God in time, Holiness, the Holy One in our midst, that create the essence of Isaiah's distinction.

Reprinted with permission from B. Davie Napier, *Time of Burning* (New York: The Pilgrim Press). Copyright © 1970 United Church Press.

Verses from Isaiah 6

1-4 *In the year that King Uzziah died I saw the Lord
sitting upon a throne, high and lifted up; and his train
filled the temple. Above him stood the seraphim; each
had six wings; with two he covered his face, with two
he covered his feet, and with two he flew. And one
called to another and said: "Holy, holy, holy is the
Lord of hosts; the whole earth is full of his glory."*

4-5 *And the foundations of the thresholds shook at the
voice of him who called, and the house was filled with
smoke.*

[The shaking of foundations, and fire and smoke
also elsewhere in the Old Testament signify the
presence of God.]

*And I said: "Woe is me! For I am lost; for I am a man of
unclean lips . . . ; for my eyes have seen the King, the
Lord of hosts!"*

[Perhaps we should read "*the* King" in contrast to
King Uzziah.]

6-7 *Then flew one of the seraphim to me, having in his
hand a burning coal which he had taken with tongs
from the altar. And he touched my mouth, and said:
"Behold, this has touched your lips; your guilt is taken
away, and your sin forgiven."*

[And this is all we know or hear of seraphim. They
appear nowhere else in the Old Testament. The
Hebrew root has to do with "burning."]

8-10 *And I heard the voice of the Lord saying, "Whom shall
I send, and who will go for us?" Then I said, "Here am
I! Send me." And he said, "Go and say to this people:*
[It seems clear in what follows that Isaiah is
looking back on the experience of his Call from a
point much later in his long ministry when it
seems to him that his own prophetic career has
served only to make his people more obdurate.]

'Hear and hear, but do not understand;
see and see, but do not perceive.'
Make the heart of this people fat,
and their ears heavy,
and shut their eyes;
lest they see with their eyes,
and hear with their ears,
and understand with their hearts,
and turn and be healed."

11   *Then I said, "How long, O Lord?" And he said:*
"Until cities lie waste
without inhabitant,
and houses without men,
and the land is utterly desolate."

(RSV)

It is Isaiah who speaks first; then the Reverend Doctor Winner; and finally, briefly, Davie Napier.

It is Isaiah speaking now, this month, this year. Not in the year that King Uzziah of Judah died—about 740 B.C. Not twenty-seven hundred years ago. But now.

I

It is the year that King Uzziah died.
That's any year—for kings, my friend, are dying;
since any child of man is child of God,
born to be free, and to subdue the earth.
My God, we go on killing kings like flies;
potential kings, the little kids that perish,
puking away their short-lived animation;
starved or exposed; or caught by rampant wars
imposed by men who would be emperors,
restraining other men from exercising
their given right to live as kings, as men.

This is the year—these are the years—when kings
are dying, sacrificed to feed the arrogance

of emperors concerned (they say) to save
(they say) the world (they say) from "commanists"
(they say). And they, these mighty emperors,
will save the world, by God, if saving means
destruction.

See the year of dying kings,
aborted births of kings, the stillborn kings—
black kings, deprived of crown, and dispossessed
of kingdom.

II

See the year of emperors
whose law and order function to preserve
the rights of emperors, and to deprive
the rights of kings, the freedom to be men.

The emperors—they come in several colors,
appear in many lands and capitals,
hold office in establishments of law
and labor, commerce, education—
the emperors deprive the kings of kingdom;
make every year a year of kingly death;
suppress the sometimes raucous stuff of freedom,
creative chaos of conflicting kings and kingdoms
in which restless, tumultuous state alone
man can emerge as man, and live as king.

III

It is the year that King Uzziah died.
I see the Lord. Well now, that's stretching things.
No man sees God, for heaven's sake. If God
is God he's not accessible to view
by any kind of pious peeping Tom—
be he prophet or priest or even saint.

If now we talk of sensing Holiness,
if we suspect an unexpected Presence;

if from the lips of seraphim not seen
before or since or, in the normal way
of apprehending, even now, we think
we hear a word of glory in the earth;
if we are sensitive to mystery;
if in the private place of our existence
we freshly sense the possibilities
of life, of new creation, restoration—
we know it has to do with dying kings,
and with our apprehension of the loss
of kingliness.

        It is against the fact
of death, the scene of human unfulfillment;
it is against the knowledge of our woe,
the recognition of the sucking vacuum
of all our inhumanity that we,
among the world's sophisticated folk,
have intimations that our world of death,
our place of bleak unholiness, can be
invaded by the glory of the Holy.

This is the year of King Uzziah's death,
and these are times when kingliness is crushed,
when man, conceived to be a little less
than God, is less than man. This is a time
of shaking of foundations—and a time
of burning.

IV

        When the kingdom of mankind
is not a kingdom, but for most a prison,
a form of tight, inhibiting restraint
of realization of humanity;
when man's existence, when the very temple
that is his total corporate habitation
is shaken to its deepest understructure,
its long-submerged supports, its cornerstones;

145

and when his house, this earthly tabernacle,
is filled with smoke of man's incineration—
his burning anger, bitterness, frustration,
his burning hate, humiliation, hunger,
his burning pride, consuming self-concern,
his burning psyche and his burning flesh—
When all of this occurs, and it is now,
it is a time of Calling . . . and a time
of certainty that Holiness is here.

V

Of course, you may deny all this, insist
you do not read this season of our life
this way. You may be one who hears and hears
but does not understand, who sees and sees,
refusing to perceive. You may deny
the shaking of the world's foundations, smoke
from human conflagrations. You may be
an emperor, contemptuous of Kings,
of men who would be men. If this is true,
your temple is a miniature illusion,
your sanctuary is a private place
complete with garden for a ghostly walk,
an unreal, insubstantial tête-à-tête
among the dew-kissed roses. You will let me
wish you and your non-Jesus Jesus well.

The time of burning is the time of calling.
The knowledge, the acknowledgment, that man
is reeling in a deeply shaken world
opens the eye and ear to Holiness,
to Glory in the earth. The awful sense
that we are all unclean, immersed in death,
makes possible the vision of the King.

VI

Some see the vision in another way,
Some read this matter very differently.

I yield the floor to Reverend Doctor Winner,
no doubt of Norman stock, invincible.

"What is this talk of death? Isaiah lies.
To be a king, a living king, one has
but to confront oneself with fortitude.
One must resolve to think in positive,
affirmative, American, red-white-
and-blue, noncommunist, nonradical,
[nonbiblical?], autohypnotic terms.

"Isaiah's call should read: It was the year
that King Uzziah died. Poor man, he failed
to use the formula sufficiently.
He failed to tell himself repeatedly,
feet squarely planted, shoulders back, facing
his mirror with a smile, 'Kings never die!'
How should Isaiah's calling read? The year
of fire and death; the shaking of the Temple
of human habitation; burning time
in human history—maybe. But this
is not for me. It is for lesser men.
For I am in Jerusalem a man
of privilege, admired, accepted, loved;
a man of parts, acquainted with the ways
of royalty. As one to whom men turn
in hope, I am upheld in high esteem.

"Why should I bear the griefs and carry sorrows
of other men? Why let myself be hurt?
Why carry wounds of other men's transgressions;
and why be bruised for their iniquities?

"Or why, indeed, be called? I'll be the Caller!
Let other men protest of unclean lips
and take for cure the purifying fire.
I'm not about to be an errand boy
of Holiness!

"It is the year of death
and I resolve that with the help of me,
myself, and my resources, I will live.
I will believe in me, myself, and so
should you. Now, suddenly, I see myself
upon a lofty throne. I know my strength.
I stamp upon my mind indelibly
the vivid image of my own success.
And it is I who say, 'Who now will go
for us?' and God responds, 'I'm here. Use me.'"

VII

So runs the version of the call revised
by Doctor Winner, and cordially endorsed
by clean, white, Anglo-Saxon Protestants
who think they have it made, or want to think
they have it made, by virtue of their own,
their very private merit; who believe
that God who knows a good thing when he sees it
is standing by them ready to respond,
and make of any untoward situation
an instant Camelot—for them, of course,
and other knights and ladies of the faith.

VIII

These are the awful days of dying kings,
when men, born to be men, are less than men.
The sacrificial altar fire is burning.
Foundations shake. And we are all unclean.
But if we listen with prophetic ears,
within the smoke-filled temple of our world
the seraphim are calling, burning calls
to burning, strangely not of death but life,
not of despair, but hope, and not of shame
but glory. Burning cries of holiness,
invading all of man's unholiness,
as Christ, the son of God, the son of man,

the king—unceasingly invading time,
incessantly enduring crucifixion—
proclaims the ultimate but, in a sense,
already present rule of righteousness.

IX

If you are burned by burning, intimate
with altar fires; if your own lips are seared
with burning coals from sacrificial altars;
if crucifixion—once for all in Christ
or in the bloody stream of human history—
if crucifixion of the son of man
fully impinges on your consciousness,
then you will not be able to escape
the Calling of the Caller; you will know
that you are called, called irresistibly,
without a word of promise of success;
called out against insuperable odds
to go and speak and work and live, in faith
that judgment must be finally redemptive,
that fire ultimately purifies,
that burning is for cleansing and forgiveness,
that love and righteousness and holiness
in fact pervade this shattered habitation.

And you and I are called to live in love
and affirmation of a burning world,
in confidence that corporate guilt is purged,
our corporate want of cleanness is forgiven;
that even if the smoke is never cleared
a Holiness invades our wanton violence
and Glory fills the anguish of our times.

X

The year that King Uzziah died: a time
of burning, time of shaking, time of calling.

"Whom shall I send and who will go for us?"
And I say, trembling like a slender reed
before the hurricane, in hope alone
of love and affirmation, confidence—
I say, "I think I'm here. Send me."

ALLAN M. PARRENT

The Humanity
of the Call of God

Scripture: Isaiah 6:1-8; Luke 5:1-11

There are a few indications in contemporary culture that
the sense of God's otherness, God's transcendence, and
God's holiness has not been lost entirely, but for the most
part words like "majesty," "transcendence," "the holy,
"wonder," and "awe" are words that we do not hear much
either in the mainline churches or in evangelical religion.
Nor do these words represent experiences that are felt
much in our secular society.

John Macquarrie writes, "One of the rather obvious and
unfortunate features of the history of theology, especially
in the modern period, has been the tendency to go to
extremes in stressing either the immanence of God at the
expense of his transcendence or vice versa."

After the strong emphasis by the last theological
generation on God as wholly other and on the infinite
qualitative distinction between Creator and creatures, we
seem now in reaction to have come to the other end of the
pendulum swing as may be seen in the late "death-of-God"
theology and in the strong this-worldly emphasis of
"secular theology."

Perhaps the time has come for the pendulum to swing
again, at least part of the way. Perhaps in our aweless age,
where technology can always find the answer even to its
self-generated problem and where for man-come-of-age

the impossible takes just a little longer, what our materially blessed but spiritually depleted society needs most is precisely a recovery of transcendence, a rebirth of wonder and awe, a revival of some sense of what Rudolph Otto called the numinous or the holy, a reminder of our finite creatureliness.

This is certainly not a call for a retreat to the safety of otherworldliness and contemplation or an abandonment of the more risky, secular, immanent, this-worldly, here-and-now emphasis of recent Christian social concern. But it is to ask if we have not too rigidly separated these two emphases of the Christian life once again in our culture. And it is also to suggest with Martin Marty that recent "secular theology, with its sometimes cozy sense of at-homeness in the world as it is or was, is really more safe than the upsetting, offbeat unbalancing talk about transcendence."

After all, it was the acculturated segment of the German Church that caved in to Nazism, while the Confessing Church with its strong sense of a transcendent God stood in defiance of that particularly gross manifestation of idolatry.

This is not a call for "mere transcendence." Rather it is a call for union of an awareness of transcendence with prophetic passion.

It is significant that awe, wonder, and a sense of the holy and of the majesty that transcends man are precisely the feelings one experiences in reading our scripture lessons. In describing his call Isaiah says he saw the Lord, sitting on a throne, high and lifted up. Seraphim sang, "Holy is the Lord of Hosts, the whole earth is full of his glory." The foundations of the thresholds shook, and the house was filled with smoke. Seldom do we find the otherness of God so clearly set forth in scripture or do we sense so vividly his all-embracing holiness. This is not the benevolent, easy-going Father or the grand old Man of culture religion.

The total contrast which Isaiah experienced between that which is holy, qualitatively different, wholly other, transcendent, and everything else, Isaiah and his people included, could elicit from Isaiah nothing other than the words: "Woe is me! For I am lost; for I am a man of unclean lips, and I dwell in the midst of a people of unclean lips; for my eyes have seen the King, the Lord of hosts!" (RSV). The real manifestation of God in his holiness and majesty and power, the divine epiphany, forces Isaiah to see himself as he really is and his people as they really are. This evokes a response akin to that of Job: "I had heard of thee by the hearing of the ear, but now my eye sees thee; therefore I despise myself, and repent in dust and ashes" (RSV).

But a strange thing happened to Isaiah. It was the primitive belief that no man could see God and live. In the deeper spiritual sense that is true and was shown to be true here. But Isaiah did not experience physical death. Rather he became a new person. In the language of biblical imagery the Seraphim purify the lips of the prophet with a burning coal. Isaiah is told that his guilt is taken away and his sins are forgiven. The old man has died, and by the power of divine grace Isaiah becomes a new creation, a twice-born man. God shows himself to be not only holy and transcendent but also gracious and forgiving, the giver of new life.

It is only then that Isaiah hears the voice of God for the first time, saying: "Whom shall I send? Who will go for us?" And it is only then, after the experience of deep self-awareness as a man of unclean lips, after the contrasting experience of God's grace and forgiveness, and after the experience of becoming a new creation, that Isaiah was able to both hear the call of God and to respond, "Here am I, send me."

God's call is recognized and answered not by those who consider themselves worthy of and ready for such a call but by those who know themselves to be unworthy and unready but nevertheless called; not by those who rely on their own moral strength and moral superiority but by those who know their own weakness and sin and also the grace and forgiveness of a holy and loving God.

In the gospel lesson, which tells of the call of Peter and

others to be fishers of men, we see a similar contrast between holiness and sinfulness, power and powerlessness. Here again, as the catch of fish increases and the nets begin to break and the boats sink, we have the confrontation of finite and sinful men with that which is holy, divine, and qualitatively different. Here again we have the contrast between man and God. Here again we have the human inability to respond in any way except as Peter did: "Depart from me, for I am a sinful man, O Lord." Here again we have the divine initiative graciously seeking to quiet fears, to forgive, and then to call men to discipleship. And here again we have the response of men. After experiencing transcendent holiness and otherness, after experiencing a sincere conviction of sinfulness, and after experiencing grace and forgiveness, they are then able to hear the call of the Lord and to accept that call to be fishers of men. They left everything, we are told, and followed him.

But then it is not Peter or the others who will catch men or save men. It was not Isaiah who accomplished what he was sent to do after his call. They were and knew themselves to be only agents and channels of the work which God would accomplish through them. They were still unclean, sinful men as they confessed themselves to be, limited, self-centered, and qualitatively different from the transcendent holiness of Deity by which they had been confronted and grasped. Yet they were also different.

Isaiah was different because he had encountered not the benevolent and easy-going Father but the one who sits above the circle of the earth. Peter was different because he had encountered not the pale Galilean of popular imagination but the one he himself felt compelled to address as Lord. Their confrontation with what was holy, transcendent, and qualitatively different had resulted in a new level of self-awareness. They saw vividly what they were and what they were not. But it also resulted in a new level of God-awareness. They experienced the fact that he who is holy is also loving, he who is righteous is also merciful, and he who is all-powerful calls men to help him as his partners and co-workers.

Barth in his *Humanity of God* speaks of God's "sovereign togetherness" with man: "Who God is and what he is in his Deity he proves and reveals not in a vacuum as the partner of man, though of course the absolutely superior partner."

There is a lesson here for us as Christians. We, like Isaiah and Peter, are called to be partners of God, even co-creators with him in a world he continues to create, judge, and redeem. But this must always be on his terms and not ours, doing his tasks and not ours, following his agenda and not ours. For those in the ministry there must be a realization that ultimately it is his ministry and not ours. A partnership with God which forgets whose terms, tasks and agenda are primary, which forgets whose ministry it is, and which forgets whose service it is in which alone one finds perfect freedom—such a partnership will soon run into bankruptcy.

One of the dangers of our aweless age and its sometimes overly optimistic celebration of man-come-of-age is that the junior partner will attempt to take over the firm. A God who is no longer transcendent, who is only immanent and man writ large, will soon be replaced by a God created by man, in the image of man, and in the control of man. Such a God inspires no awe, no conviction, no commitment, and no discipleship. The call to serve such a God may be accepted without fear of excessive demands or challenge.

But for Isaiah and Peter, God's call and their response came only after a confrontation with that which was holy, qualitatively different, and transcendent. The experience made them more aware of their own weakness and unworthiness. Such an experience might at first be thought to be a deterrent to accepting and challenge. How can added awareness of one's shortcomings act as a spur to commitment and action? But the result was just the opposite. For their experience also showed them a gracious, forgiving, loving, and empowering God, a God both transcendent and with us, a God who challenged them to be what they were created to be, and a God who also promised them that he would sustain and empower them to do what he called them to do.

When we say to this God, "Here am I, send me," we enter a life that makes more demands than we can possibly fulfill. The best intentions, the best education, and the best equipment cannot fill the gap. But through Christ we are assured that he whom God calls, God will also sustain and empower to do the task he is called to do. Some may be empowered to interpret the signs of our times to God's people, if that is what is needed. Others may be empowered to see much less, if that is the job we are called by God to do. The important thing, however, is to know the God who calls and to know him both as transcendent God and incarnate Lord. We can then respond with ultimate confidence that the one who calls can and will work through us to accomplish his loving purposes. For the one who is holy and whose ways are not our ways is also the one who through Christ has shown himself to be God for us and God with us.

CHARLES L. RICE

"Watch, Therefore . . ."

Mark 13:32-37

On a Monday in late November I joined step with the
          commuters who hustle down our street to the
          station five mornings a week,
  and come dragging their briefcases up the hill, some of
  them, long after children have gone to bed.
As usual, the people on the 7:16, headed for mid-Manhattan
          or the World Trade Center, most of them, were as
          quiet as old friends at breakfast,
  settled into their familiar routines:
    reading, sleeping,
      scribbling on top of a briefcase like a schoolchild
      who hasn't done homework,
or just looking out the window, listening to the clickety-
      clack.
You could hardly help noticing how nicely turned out they
          were,
  fresh from the shower,
    Oxford cloth, pinstripes, and tweed.

Then I spied the first sign of the season, up front, on the ad
          space beside the door.
The poster shows a child's sled, wooden, with red trim,
          sitting in a circle of snow against a dark
          background, and below, the question:

Used by permission of Charles L. Rice.

REMEMBER WHEN THIS WAS THE ONLY THING
YOU WANTED IN THE WHOLE WORLD?
                              —Johnnie Walker

There wasn't any sign on that sedate train that anyone else
            saw it. But as the good old Erie-Lackawanna
            rattled and rolled toward New York and another
            day's work, I wondered if some of my fellow
            travelers,
    deep into their trenchcoats and the *Wall Street Journal,*
    didn't find their eyes, too,
wandering now and again to that Flexible Flyer.

But who needs a nostalgic trip?
That's exactly what we are likely to get at this time of year,
            and just what we need:
    when Christmas wrap now costs $5.00 a roll,
        more and more families face the holidays broken,
and the world has more nuclear weapons than this time
            last year. So we are supposed to remember how
            great it was when all our hopes and fears were
            no bigger than what we would or wouldn't get
            for Christmas?

Somehow we have more respect for people who just get up
            and go to work,
    take this world for what it is,
and *cope,* for themselves and the people who depend upon
            them.
That red-faced man bent over his briefcase with the
            morning flying by the train window,
    or the trim woman glued to the stock page as if her life
    depended upon it—
we understand people like that,
who are trying, despite all odds,
to make it.
Is there any other way?
If the old sled triggers anything in them, it is probably that
            they haven't really thought about Christmas
            presents yet.

At the same time this season puts the question to us:

What are we, even while we hurry and scratch and cope, looking for, living on?

Watch! says Mark.

Keep in mind, says Jesus, those servants who do their work but keep an eye out.

In Jesus' story, the landowner goes away and leaves his employees in charge of the estate.

Living in the kingdom is like that, he says.

Watch, therefore—for you do not know when the master of the house will come, in the evening, or at midnight, or at cockcrow, or in the morning—lest he come suddenly and find you asleep. And what I say to you, I say to all: Watch. (Mark 13:35-27 RSV)

Now some have understood that to mean that the world of stocks and bonds,

lawyers and dentists,

people off to work and sleepy kids dillydallying to school,

gardeners and housepainters,

doesn't really matter.

We're supposed to live on tiptoe—our eyes on the skies—and, in the extreme,

give up on this world,

throw in the towel,

and find some hilltop to watch for his coming.

There is that bumper sticker:

"If Jesus comes, someone grab my steering wheel."

Not a bad metaphor for a certain way of being—or not being—in the world:

someone driving around solo in an air-conditioned, sound-proofed, high-powered car, insulated by mobility and ready energy from the groaning environment, just passing through to glory.

But in Jesus' story the servants do their work while keeping a sharp eye out.

God's kingdom is here already—

159

in work to do and commuters out the door with hardly
time for breakfast,
not to mention scanning the skies,
more interested in Dow Jones or the price of gas.
But this is there too: keep on looking.
Keep on expecting.
The trains keep to their schedules.
We come and go, our eyes fixed on today's news, and it may
be that the world *is* too much with us . . .

> . . . late and soon,
> Getting and spending, we
> lay waste our powers.

But occasionally, over the heads of our brothers and
sisters, we are brought up short, even by the ad
writer's pitch, to realize that we are in fact
living not on today's news alone,
or merely on our cleverness or prowess,
but we are finally—are we not?—living on *hope*.
And the faster we go, the more we try to distract ourselves
from it, the more we betray what it is that we
are looking for:

DO YOU REMEMBER WHAT IT IS THAT YOU
WANT MORE THAN ANYTHING ELSE IN THE
WHOLE WORLD?

Are you looking for it?
Watching and waiting?

Paul Tillich, in his sermon for Advent, said:
"Although waiting is *not having,* it is also *having*."
The fact that we wait for something shows that in some
way we already possess it. The apocalyptic
visionary sees the future from the vantage
point of one who has *already* to depend upon
God's mercy as the world's foundations shake.
Jesus, and Mark his gospeler—like us—take up the image
that can say this for us,

that we watch and wait for what is already here with us, present to us in our doldrums and in our anxieties even— Someone has painted on the railway trestle near the station, in foot-high letters, SATISFACTION —and in the glimpse we get, here and there, of our deepest hopes, for ourselves and for the world.

The one for whom we wait is already here.

Karen was a student of mine at Union Theological Seminary a few years back. While she was living and studying in New York City, her newly lawyered husband had hung up his shingle in Harrisburg; they saw each other only on weekends. She described to our class what Fridays were like, when John came into Penn Station by train, in time for a late supper. "Well, I usually get up early on Friday to clean the apartment before coming up here to school. Then after classes, I make a kind of safari down Broadway. I stop for groceries, a bottle of wine, and tuck some flowers under my arm. And when I get home I have just enough time to get myself and supper ready. Then John comes home." Karen went on: "The funny thing about it is, that from morning until he gets there, I have this strange feeling that he is already with me. Not really, but *really*."

If I had to come up with my own images of that—
    this having while not having,
        waiting while working,
            watching for the one who is already with us
    (could the picture Jesus paints of the servants at work while waiting for their master be a friendly scene, not so much threat as seriousness about taking care of something important to a friend?)
—they would be two.

First would be a circle of friends who come together around the table of thanksgiving,
    to remember him,
        in bread and wine to show forth under these simple signs his long-suffering faithfulness and love,

his death,
until he come.
That would be the first image, where he is *present,* as we
say,
present to all that we know of life,
its demand as daily as bread,
its joy as much a gift as wine,
and all that can come to us,
even to the hour of our death,
and yet to come.
The one who is to come in clouds, as we say, is here,
in bread which we have baked,
among these motley saints.

The second, again, took place on a train, on the same old E
& L, with its wicker seats and peeling paint,
and in warm weather, as it was on this
particular day,
black wire fans like the one that turned slowly in your
grandmother's parlor.

It was the homeward-bound commuter, the 6:17.
Every seat was taken, and I had to stand in the back.
The doors and windows were open, for the breeze,
the shades halfway down against the late afternoon sun.
Even the old train seemed to feel the early summer heat as
we set out toward the short hills and, beyond,
the valley towns.

The scene was multicolored pastel—most of the jackets
were in the overhead racks—
and strangely quiet:
people napping, reading, daydreaming.
The car was swaying gently, and from where I stood, the
eighty heads and shoulders could have been
choreographed—
all moving together to the rhythm of the train.
Coming from who knows what kind of day,
and going home to God only knows what,
not even talking to each other,

we were for a moment all dancing together through the
               Hoboken yards, the wastelands that once were
               meadows,
   through Newark, and right on to Summit, the first stop.

It was a glimpse—they steal up on us when we least
               expect—of what we are waiting for,
   and of what is here already,
     here and there,
       now and then:
the time when God's will shall be done on earth, and in our
               very hearts, as in heaven.
When we see it,
   our deepest hopes and fears are met,
in the one who was, and is, and is to come. Amen.

JOHN A. T. ROBINSON

A Unique Christ

What future for a unique Christ? It is a surprisingly modern question. It's safe to say that even when I was an undergraduate it would not have rated in the top ten. It was something that if you were a Christian you simply tended to take for granted. We weren't still quite with Fielding's Pastor Thwackum and his splendid simplicities. "When I speak of religion," he said, "I mean the Christian religion. And when I speak of the Christian religion, I mean the Protestant religion. And when I speak of the Protestant religion, I mean the Church of England." But in practice one got away with talking about "our incomparable religion" (or "liturgy," or whatever) because in ignorance it never received comparison or in insolence was placed beyond it.

But now the situation is very different. In fact even to claim that Jesus Christ is unique or final sounds arrogant, and most young people, I suppose, would begin by assuming the opposite. Indeed many Christians seriously wonder in what sense if any they should even try to defend it.

There has been a challenge on at least two fronts. First, and most obviously, from other religions. Unlike our fathers, we in England now actually live in a multi-faith society, and in many cities we have to take this into account in our educational syllabus. Hindus and Buddhists, Sikhs and Moslems, are our neighbors, and every variety of

A sermon preached by the Rt. Rev. Dr. J. A. T. Robinson in Trinity College Chapel, Cambridge, October 15, 1978. Used by permission of Dr. Robinson.

Eastern wisdom is on offer in the underground. Gurus come and gurus go, and even the divinity faculty is not confined to Christian theology. We cannot go on talking about Christ as in the days when Christians and even humanists had it to themselves.

The other challenge is more subtle but if anything more profound. Jungian psychology, for instance, which is the most sympathetic to religion, speaks very positively of the Christ-figure as an archetype of the self. Yet why confine this to Jesus or tie it to that particular bit of history? If I were born in India or China I would image it very differently. Man has developed a rich store of symbols. That of the Christ crucified and risen may, as Jung says, be a very profound one. But why make it exclusive? For many people, other images, of the mandala or the lotus, will speak more compellingly.

Well, in what sense if any should a thoughtful Christian want to maintain that Jesus was unique?

First of all, here are two senses which I think we can rule out.

(1) The weak sense in which each and every one of us is unique, an unrepeatable individual. That is very mysterious but not very significant, though it *is* important to say this of Jesus against some forms of traditional Christian doctrine which have stressed that he was man at the expense of his being genuinely and in every sense a man.

(2) The opposite extreme is to say that he was absolutely unique *in kind*. He after all was the Son of God. He may have lived like a man, he may have been like us in every respect (except sin), but he entered our human scene from without, like a cuckoo born into the human nest. He was an anomalous exception—a heavenly being *becoming* a man rather than a regular product of the evolutionary process like every other member of the species *homo sapiens*.

Now one can dress up this claim in all sorts of ways, and it is at the heart of what many Christians would say was of the essence of the Christian faith, but I don't think you can get round the conclusion that this is presenting a Christ who was unique because he was abnormal. And the corollary of this, if you press it, is that he is of very doubtful relevance for the rest of us. He didn't start where we start, and I believe in fact that it undermines the gospel rather than defends it. If this is what is meant by the uniqueness of Jesus as the Christ then I think it is rightly under question and it is healthy that, both from inside and outside the church, traditional presentations of the doctrine of the incarnation and person of Christ should have come under examination. If *The Myth of God Incarnate* had done it better and if its answer, *The Truth of God Incarnate,* had even heard the question, some useful clearing of the ground might have been effected. Instead I fear both sides have queered the pitch. But I don't want to rake over that rubble.

Let me state the only sense in which I would want to defend the uniqueness of Christ. And this is that Jesus is unique because he alone of all mankind of whom we have any external evidence or internal experience was truly normal. He was *the* son of man, *the* son of God, the Proper Man, who lived in a relation to God and his fellow men in which we are all called to live but fail to live. This doesn't mean that he had everything or was everything (you mention it, he had it), but that here was a man who uniquely embodied the relationship with God for which man was created. In this man, God was reflected, as John puts it, in a simile from family life, as in an only son of his father—he who had seen him had seen the Father. Or as Paul puts it, he was the image of the invisible God, the perfect reproduction, as opposed to the distorting mirror, of his fullness, his glory. Unlike the contributors to *The Myth* volume, I would want strongly to retain and insist upon the category of "incarnation." For in this man, the Christian gospel dares to assert, we see the Word, the Logos, the self-expressive activity of God in all nature and history, what God was and is, enmanned as far as human nature can contain it in an actual historical individual who is bone of our bone, flesh of our flesh—the only truly normal son of man and son of God.

That is in all conscience a tremendous claim. But before

going on to say how I would defend it, let me refine it further against misunderstanding.

To believe that God is best defined in Jesus is not to believe that God is confined to Jesus. On the contrary, as John makes clear in his prologue, the life and the light focused in this man is the life with which everything is alive and the light which enlightens every man coming into the world. Jesus is not the exclusive revelation or act of God. The Bible itself insists that he has not left himself without witness everywhere, that at sundry times and in divers manners he has been speaking to his world. As the book of Wisdom so beautifully put it of the divine Wisdom, well before the birth of Jesus, "age after age she enters into holy souls and makes them God's friends and prophets." The many-faceted splendor and the strange and often dark shapes under which God has been apprehended and worshiped are becoming more familiar to us the more we know both of comparative religion and depth psychology. The Christ-image is infinitely bigger and richer—and more disturbing—than what Christians under the influence both of Catholic triumphalism and of Protestant particularism have made of it, by drawing a tight little circle around the historical Jesus (or rather, their image of him) and calling it the whole of God. *If* Jesus as the Christ is unique, it is not because he is exclusive of any other revelation or the denial of any other saving activity of God but because he is uniquely inclusive—the concentration as in a burning-glass of the light and the love that is at work everywhere, enabling one to make better sense of it than any other figure in history. As Paul puts it again from his experience, "in him all things cohere and hang together." In the title of a book on Indian Christian theology, he "is unique *and* universal."

I would call myself a Christian because I would in all humility dare to make the same claim. It is not because I don't see any light or anything of God in all these ot^h figures or images: on the contrary I am more especially as a result of my visit to the East last y⌐ one-eyed and blinkered we have allowed become. I need these other figures and images to complete, clarify, and correct, to use Reinhold Niebuhr's formula, what comes to me through my own tradition. It is rather that what I see in Jesus as the Christ, and not only in the thirty years of his earthly life but in what Augustine called the *Totus Christus* filling and reconciling the entire cosmos, that which incorporates and integrates more of my experience than any of the other focal figures or archetypal images.

Since I have mentioned Jung, let me use a category of his that I think provides a crucial test of this claim—the "shadow." This stands for all those elements in experience that are not in themselves evil but which we would rather not have to live with or acknowledge, the things about ourselves or our world that we repress or project on to others—all the dark aspects of life we would rather reject than integrate. Maturity, wholeness, individuation, he said, comes from being able to incorporate and integrate the shadow. But what we are tempted to do is disown it and to project images of God or the Christ-figure as archetypes of the self from which these aspects of reality, without us or within, are hived off on to some anti-body, like the Devil or Anti-Christ. And Christians, said Jung, have been as guilty of this as anyone, leaving themselves with a God or Christ-figure that rejects so much in experience, the suffering, the impersonal, and, in the case of chauvinist males, the feminine, instead of taking it up and creatively dealing with it. That is why "the unacceptable face of Christianity," to be seen so often in church history, constantly stands in need of completing, clarifying, and correcting by the truth that can come through the dialogue with other religions and indeed with psychology and humanism and Marxism and light from any other source.

But when all has been said that has to be said—and even Jesus himself, as the Author to the Hebrews boldly says, had to be perfected, made whole by the things that he suffered—I am persuaded that this particular model of the Christ incorporates the shadow, enables the antinomies of experience to cohere and hang together, more creatively than any other. Thus in its central and distinctive mystery of the cross and resurrection, Christianity integrates and transfigures the light and the dark sides more profoundly than in the coexistence, for instance, within Hinduism of Krishna and Kali, the figures of dalliance and destruction; it deals with the problems of suffering, and above all of sin, more radically and dynamically than the impassive serenity of the Buddha, however moving; and for all its sanctioning, especially in Protestantism, of the great white male upon the throne, and its current rejection in Catholicism of women-priests, it incorporates the female more fully than either the patriarchal religions of Judaism or (especially) Islam.

I make this claim with great humility and open-endedness— without presuming to say that it *must* look like this to others. Yet for all I receive and still more need to receive from elsewhere, I would not be honest to my apprehension of the truth if I did not also want to insist that for me that revelation of God as Father in the cross of Christ and the disclosure of man's destiny, as one of the early Christian Fathers put it, "as in a son," represents the interpretation of the less than personal in experience by the personal in a manner and to a degree that I do not see anywhere else. And I would echo the testimony of a Christian theologian who has reflected on these questions as deeply and as long as any of our generation, Norman Pittenger: "For myself I believe that the finality of Christ is nothing other than his decisive disclosure that God is suffering, saving and ecstatic love. Surely you cannot get anything more final than that. But there may be many different approaches to this, many different intimations, adumbrations and preparations."

Yet for the New Testament itself, Jesus, and his resurrection, are but the firstfruits of the harvest to come, the "leading shoot," in Teilhard de Chardin's term, of the new humanity. Indeed in the words of an Indian Christian theologian, which echo the old church Father Irenaeus, "the Incarnation is as much about what man is to become as what God has become." The finality of Christ is not a misleading phrase only if we remember that for Paul "the perfect man," like "the last Adam," is a description not of the historical Jesus but of that new spiritual humanity into which mankind has but begun to be built. If for Christians Jesus is of unique and definitive significance (a less misleading world than final), it is not because he is the last word beyond which it is impossible to say anything or some static norm, like the standard meter, against which every other has for ever to be lined up, but because they believe, as I believe, that he offers the best clue we inhabitants of planet earth have to what Blake called "the human form divine" or Tennyson dared to speak of as "the Christ that is to be."

ROBERT H. SCHULLER

Turn Your Scars into Stars!

Out of your weakness shall come strength
—Hebrews 11:34

That is like saying where the bone was broken, it knitted, welded, healed, and became stronger than at any other point in the shaft . . .

It is like saying where the flesh was cut and the tissue healed, the skin mended, and a scar formed, it became tougher than at any other point on the surface of the body.

A guide said to me one time some years ago in the Netherlands as we walked across the dike: "See that huge concrete plug? That is where we had a leak one time and the sea rushed in and many people perished, but we plugged it with concrete, steel-reinforced it; it will never break there again."

> *"Where you are weak, there you will*
> *be made strong."*

A doctor said to me one time as he pointed to a nurse walking down the hallway, "She is the best nurse we have. How she works! She is so dedicated." Then, as an afterthought he said, "It is because when she was a teenager she spent ten months on her back in this hospital."

I keep hearing compliments about my secretary, Lois Wendell, especially from people who are going through problems like cancer operations. I suppose it is because Lois had the first of several cancer operations twelve or thirteen years ago.

Turn your scars into stars! Your hurts can be turned into halos!

> *Out of your weakness can come*
> *strength.*

There is a key principle here: If you want to live an emotionally healthy and happy life you have to know how to handle the hurts that come. There are, if I may suggest, six or seven forms of hurts that may strike us: There is such a thing, for instance, as being hurt by your friends. And we all know what it is like, I suppose, to be hurt by an enemy. There is a third type of hurt and that is the self-inflicted wound that you inflict upon yourself and later you hate yourself for what you did to yourself. Hurts from friends, from enemies, from self-inflicted hurts; and there are others that you can only say life threw at you.

So the bridge collapsed and somebody made a mistake and you got hurt. You really can't pin the blame on anyone, not even yourself; at a time like that it is always a temptation to blame God. Be careful! The odds are that some human being committed a mistake and that is why it happened.

Then, there are those hurts that God causes. A loved one is taken home. God took him and you are hurt. Yet when you married him, God never promised you how long you could have him; it was simply for better or for worse, 'til death do us part. It might have been a day, it might have been a week, maybe a month, perhaps a year, maybe even ten years. God made no promises.

> *Turn your weakness into*
> *strength.*

The book of Hebrews advises! How do you do that? I would suggest it could be done with four principles—four things to keep in mind to handle life's hurts:

(1) Don't curse them;
(2) Don't rehearse and nurse them;
(3) Disperse them (I will show you how);
Finally,
(4) Reverse them! Turn them inside out until the hurt becomes a halo, and the scar becomes a star!

(1) DON'T CURSE THEM!

I hear it all the time: "See her," they say; "she has been drinking a lot ever since she lost her husband." Or they point to him and they say, "You know, he has been going downhill ever since the boy died." Or they say: "Oh, he dropped out of high school when he was a senior because he didn't make the football team. That did it." Or they point to her and say: "I think I'm going to have to let her go; she is just not doing her work. Ever since she didn't get the promotion, she hasn't been much good to the company."

(2) DON'T REHEARSE THEM AND NURSE THEM!

I had a lady call in my office this week, a dear friend of mine. Her husband passed away two years ago. The poor, dear soul—how I wished she had come in sooner, one and a half years ago, or at least one year ago. She waited so long, two long, suffering, painful years, crying inside alone, killing herself with grief.

She had been rehearsing how it all happened! How he was acting eight weeks before he had the heart attack; six weeks before, four weeks and three weeks. Then she recalled what he did the week before the attack and, finally, the fatal morning. She had been rehearsing the scene over and over again. Then she said, as she opened her large purse and got out her billfold: "I have something here that I always carry with me. I wanted to know just why he died. So I asked the doctor, couldn't they have tried electric shock to start the heart, or opened it and massaged it, or something?" The doctor gave her a very technical, clinical definition of how he died. She copied that down on a piece of paper. She said, "I copied it down on this piece of paper and I carry it with me all the time."

She showed it to me. I don't remember it exactly, but it was something to this effect: "Your husband's condition started because of an inner problem in the arteries which became clogged, then blood clots formed, and finally one of the large clots got so large that it closed off the whole passage so that the blood could no longer flow into the heart. When that happened the valve closed off and then an enormous pain came. Then the lungs no longer were able to expand and then he died from a failure of oxygen, et cetera." It was all clinically written on this piece of paper!

I almost cried for her, because I love her very much. Well, I had a prayer with her, and God performed a healing there in my study. I said to her, "Now, I want to say one final thing before you leave. One last piece of advice." She said, "Sure, Reverend, anything you say." I said, "I want you to take that piece of paper and I want you to tear it up and throw it away. Don't ever look at it again." She said, "Really? Do you think that is what I should do?" I said, "I know that is what you should do." She said, "Okay, Reverend, I'll do that." And I am sure she did.

(3) DISPERSE YOUR HURTS!

Don't nurse and rehearse them, but disperse them. Here's how:

You probably can't help it when the hurt comes, but you can help it if the hurt lasts. Through the power of God and through the power of prayer you can handle any hurt. I know this is true. But you have to pray the right way.

A friend of mine was having a problem with a competitor, and all kinds of negative emotions were coming in. I suggested to him to pray about it. He said, "What do I pray? Do I pray that the guy will succeed?" I said, "Well, I don't know, just pray that God will tell you what to pray. Ask God what to pray for."

This week he told me, "I woke up at two o'clock in the morning and I had the prayer." I said, "What was it?" He said, "This was the prayer:

"Dear God, make that person into exactly the person you want him to be and cause his business to develop just the way you would like to see it develop. Amen."

My friend continued, "That just completely cured me. Now, if that guy's business succeeds, I can't possibly be angry about it. I know God wants it to go. Of course, if he goes bankrupt—well, I will be able to face that, too." He was very sincere:

"God, make him the person you want him to be and cause his business to develop the way you want it to develop."

A few years ago, Archbishop Fulton Sheen spoke about hurts in this pulpit. You know that the Archbishop has had some personal deep hurts. He said, **"I was able to find peace when I realized that ultimately nothing ever happened unless God at least permitted it."** What a profound statement!

Normally, to really get rid of your hurts you have to look deep into your own self. Somehow you have to find at what point you, yourself, were at fault.

I have had experience with hurts . . . like the time I thought I was an innocent victim. In retrospect, I must admit I did some stupid things, said some things in a most audacious way and provoked some of my problems, I am sure.

If you have a problem with a person, I am sure it is not one hundred percent the other person's fault. The hardest and the most healing word in the Bible is the word repent. That may be what you need to do.

Are you suffering from a hurt that is self-inflicted? Do you hate yourself for what you have done? Maybe you are cheating on your wife, or your wife is cheating on you; or you are stealing from your employer; or you are dishonest and you hate like Hades the man you see in the mirror.

"Oh, God," you say to yourself, "if there were just some way to tear the black page out and start over again!"

There is! That is possible! You can disperse your hurt!

Say, "Jesus Christ, take me, cleanse me, forgive me, and I know, God, if you forgive me I will be able to live with myself."

Start over fresh and clean! How do you handle your hurts? Don't curse them, don't rehearse and nurse them, disperse them.

(4) FINALLY, REVERSE YOUR HURTS.

Turn your hurts inside out and turn the problem into a project, the enemy into a friend, the hurt into a halo, the scar into a star.

The more I read about them and the more I touch great people, the more I am convinced of one thing: there is no great person alive who has not been hurt deeply.

I am so convinced of this that this week as I prepared this message, I found myself praying this amazing prayer: God, hurt me more so that I can help people more.

Years ago I was invited to preach in the Marble Collegiate Church. Dr. Peale was and still is the senior pastor of the church, but at that time the evening preacher was Dr. Daniel A. Poling. Well, I didn't know Dr. Poling, but when I came to preach in that church I didn't have my pulpit robe with me and so they looked for one that would fit me. They reached into the closet and said, "Here, Dr. Dan's should fit you." I slipped into it. It had buttons all the way down. I buttoned all the buttons, but one button came off. I slipped it into my pocket. That week I mailed it back East with a letter to Dr. Daniel A. Poling. "My apologies, sir," I wrote, "but here is a button off your robe." I got a letter back that you wouldn't believe. It was fantastic! Remember that I was just an unknown youth, only a few years away from an Iowa farm. Dr. Poling wrote: "The loss of a button is a cheap price to pay for the honor of having you wear my robe, good sir."

Later on I learned the secret of Dr. Poling's greatness. In the first World War he was a chaplain. He ran between trenches that were only one hundred yards apart. A hail of bullets went around him . . . others fell dead . . . he came out alive. In another instance he was one of four men carrying a litter. On it was a German prisoner with mangled legs. A shell exploded in the mud around him. All the others were blown to pieces, but Dan lived through it.

Then, of course you know about Clark, Dan's son. Clark was a teen-ager in a private high school which was located out of the city. He sent a telegram saying: "Dad, I am coming home this weekend. I want to see you alone. Meet me at the depot." Dr. Dan met his teen-age boy at the depot and trembled inside wondering what kind of trouble his son was in. The son said, "Now, I don't want to see Mom, I want to see you alone."

Together they went to the office at the Marble Collegiate Church and when the boy noticed there was no lock he took a chair and put it under the door knob so that nobody would interrupt their conversation.

"By this time," Dr. Dan said later, "I was really trembling inside. I sat behind my desk and my boy came and pulled a chair right up next to mine and then put his elbows on top of my desk. He put his chin in his hands and just looked. "Now," the father continued, "I made many mistakes in my life, but I didn't make a mistake here by asking what was wrong . . . I just waited.

"Finally, my boy looked up at me and said, 'Dad, tell me what do you know about God?'

"I looked back at him and said, 'What do I know about God? Very little, my son, very little. But enough to change my whole life!'

"The boy looked back and said, 'That's good enough, Daddy, that's good enough. I think I'll be a preacher like you when I grow up.' And he did. He graduated from seminary, married, and had a beautiful little baby."

Then on December 7, 1941, the bombs fell on Pearl Harbor. Clark came to his dad and said, "Dad, I am going to enlist as a chaplain. The only problem is, Dad, I think that is taking the easy way out." Dr. Dan looked at his son and said: "Don't you say that, son. I will have you know that in the first World War the most dangerous post that you could have was the post as chaplain. On a percentage basis more chaplains died in the first World War than even the infantrymen—one out of ninety-three, to be specific. If you become a chaplain, you may have your chance to die, Clark!"

Clark became a chaplain. His father was in London when he heard the news that the S.S. *Dorchester,* a troop ship with over nine hundred on board, was torpedoed off Greenland with only a handful of survivors. The rest went down with the ship. Then he read the story in the paper that one of the survivors said that the last scene, as the bow of the ship was about to slip beneath the cold waters, was the sight of four chaplains standing together on the bow, and each one was unstrapping his own life preserver and handing it to a private who jumped into the water and was saved. Then, having given their life preservers away, the four chaplains—two Protestants, a Catholic, and a Jew—all went down. One of those four was Clark Poling.

Since that time Dr. Dan's heart became so big that he wanted to take in every boy alive on planet earth. He wanted to be Dad to everybody.

Turn your scars into stars. It will make you a better person or a bitter person; it all depends on you.

Reverse them; turn your hurt into a halo.

The other day I was watching as the elevator doors opened. I had just stepped out of my office. My secretary was there. As the elevator doors opened, there was this young mother with a little girl pulling at her skirt. The mother looked busy—she seemed to be rushed, and even a little harassed. She had her hands so full that she could not help her little girl. I said to my secretary, "Who is she? What is she doing here at this time of the day?" My secretary reminded me that she is now in charge of our Helping Hand project.

She spends hours and hours at this church . . . doing what? Collecting tin cans full of soup and beans. People call into our telephone counseling center, New Hope; they call in twenty-four hours of the day. This is the first church in the United States to operate a twenty-four-hour live telephone counseling program, operated solely by members of the church. People call and tell us they have nothing. We have a policy which holds that we won't give money to people. If they have no food, we will supply them with groceries.

Now, this young mother, who is herself so busy, devotes hours every week managing this whole operation. Only a few people know how much work and time is involved. I commented on that, and my secretary said, "You remember she wrote you a letter that really moved you and impressed you a few years ago." It was a letter—I remember receiving it—that read:

Dear Dr. Schuller: I can't begin to thank you for your congregation. What wonderful Christians they are. My husband has been flat on his back in bed for months and can't work. I had a baby who became sick, and I couldn't work. The church heard about it and the ladies came and brought us breakfast, dinner and supper. They did this day after day, week after week. How can I ever repay you? How can I ever repay them?

She has found a way.

Again and again, if I look at a great person I say: Somewhere that person was hurt.

At least he got so close to seeing other people hurt that he hurt with them.

Some of you have been in the Royal Palace in Teheran, Iran. I was there for the first time this summer. I have been in royal palaces around the world, but this one was something else. There isn't anything like it, to my knowledge, any place in the world.

You step into the Royal Palace and the grand entrance is just resplendent with glittering, sparkling glass. You think for a moment that the domed ceilings and the side walls, and the columns are all covered with diamonds, until you realize that these aren't diamonds, and not cut crystal, but they are all small pieces of mirrors. The edges of a myriad little mirrors reflect the light, throwing out the colors of the rainbow. A mosaic of mirrors! Spectacular!

Here's how it happened: When the Royal Palace was planned the architects sent an order to Paris for mirrors to cover the entrance walls. The mirrors finally arrived in their crates. When they took the crates apart, all the crushed pieces spilled out! They were all smashed in

179

travel! They were going to junk them all when one creative man said, "No, maybe it will be more beautiful because they are broken."

More beautiful because it is broken? He took some of the large pieces and smashed them, and then he took all the little pieces and fitted them together like an abstract mosaic. If you see it, you will note that it is an enormous distortion in reflections; it is sparkling with rainbow diamond colors. Broken to be made beautiful!

Do you have a hurt? If you do, turn it over to God, and He will turn it inside out.

He will reverse it, and it will become a star instead of a scar in your crown!

GLEN H. STASSEN

The Time Machine

Matthew 5:9, 21-26, 38-48

One evening you and your family sit together watching a
TV movie based on H. G. Wells' *Time Machine*. It's a movie
with a serious message. It makes an impact on you. The
hero is a brilliant scientist. He works for Mega Industries,
inventing nuclear weapons. But he's worried. His evidence
indicates these weapons will kill the human race; will
make the earth so radioactive that it won't support
vegetable, animal, or human life. He presents his evidence
to his bosses: "We should not develop these weapons," he
warns. But they're interested in profits. They ignore him.
Construction goes on, with each new stage a step toward
destruction.

The scientist has been working on a new invention: a
time machine. And it works! He travels forward into the
middle of the next century. The earth is nothing but dry,
arid desert; hot, sun-baked dirt, growing nothing. The
machine's automatic warning system flashes on: "Warning: radiation 500 millirems. Fatal. Evacuate immedi-
ately." Apparently nuclear war has killed the earth and all
that is in it.

He hits the control buttons and travels farther into the
future, past the year 3000, into the thirty-first century.
There he finds an oasis-like area that has sprouted to life,
and he finds some human-like creatures called Morlocks.
In order to survive the radiation, the Morlocks have been

living underground for a thousand years and they're blind in daylight. They look like big, human-size moles, or if you have seen *Star Wars,* like large-size, strong, mean Jawas.

And then he finds some other creatures who live, for a while, above the ground. They are called the Elois, and they look more like us. On nights when the moon is dark, the Morlocks come above ground and capture an Elois or two, and eat them for meat. The Elois are the Morlock's cattle!

These two small groups, the Morlocks and the Elois, are the only remnants of the human race left on earth.

Is the story of the Time Machine a parable of our future?

What does the Sermon on the Mount say? Some people don't pay enough attention to the Sermon on the Mount because they look at it as simply some high ideals, nice but optional. They're wrong. It's realistic. It contains a realistic warning, calling us to face the reality of destruction if we don't hear Jesus' words and live by them. It says everyone who hears the words of Jesus and does not do them will be like a foolish man who built his house upon the sand; and the rain fell and the floods came; and the winds blew and beat upon that house; and it fell; and great was the fall of it. Jesus knows we need to be warned because we don't like to face the consequences of our actions. We turn our eyes away from where we are heading, and we fall into destruction. He reminds us realistically of our hypocrisy; of the log in our eye that blinds our vision; of our suicidal service of mammon (or money); of our putting our hearts in monetary treasure; of the way that leads to destruction; of judgment and the hell of fire.

The Sermon on the Mount tells us that judgment and destruction may be our end. The story of the Time Machine may indeed be the parable of where we are headed: Morlocks and Elois, hiding from residual radiation.

And so how do you answer when your son asks you, after the movie, "Dad will we ever have another war?" "Yes, I think so." "Do you think nuclear weapons might be used?"

"Yes." "Do you think they might be used here?" "Yes." "That will be bad, won't it?" "Yes, very bad."

Let's do what we usually avoid doing: Let's look realistically at where the nuclear arms race is heading. On the Pentagon's map of the United States, reprinted in the Sojourners' packet, "The Nuclear Challenge to Christian Conscience,"[1] most major cities like ours are marked with a bright color as likely targets in nuclear war. We have important industry and a large population, and there is a military base not too far away.

What does that mean? If an average-size one-megaton nuclear missile lands in the center of our city, first there will be a powerful blast that will knock down brick ranch-style homes in a circle eight miles in diameter, which is about the area enclosed by the beltway around the city. Then there will be firestorms; the heat is so hot that asphalt on the roads bursts into flames like kindling wood. This will extend twice as far as the blast, in a circle about sixteen miles in diameter. And if it is a surface burst, which causes more radiation, the radiation will be fatal for most people one hundred miles downwind.

The Office of Technology Assessment has just released a report, *The Effects of Nuclear War,* based on various government studies. It estimates conservatively that in a nuclear attack aimed at our missiles and Strategic Air Command bases, using about two-thirds of the present Russian strategic nuclear weapons, about 14 million Americans would be killed promptly. This does not include millions of lingering deaths from radiation fallout here and around the world, nor does it include interaction effects between radiation sickness, injuries, burns, disease, and lack of food, medical care, electricity or fuel, or long-range effects of ecological damage. And the radiation would drift around the earth, killing millions, mostly in the northern hemisphere.

If the Russians attack not only our nuclear weapons, but also our industrial targets, they estimate one-half to three-fourths of Americans would die in the first thirty days. It's not yet the apocalyptic total world destruction of *The Time Machine*. But it's not good.

And the nuclear arms buildup is not an unchanging reality; it is a rapidly growing monster adding weapons steadily each year, the better to devour us all. In 1962, at the time of the Cuban Missile Crisis, we were deeply worried about nuclear attack. Then the Russians had 75 intercontinental nuclear missiles to drop on us, and we had 294. Now, in 1980, they have 5,000 nuclear bombs and warheads they can drop on us, and we have 11,000.[2] If the SALT treaty fails to be ratified by our Senators, and the arms race continues uncontrolled and Russia keeps building at the present rate, by 1988 they'll have about 30,000 nuclear bombs and warheads they can drop on us! (And we'll have a similar number.)[3] That's four times as many as the Office of Technology Assessment based their estimates on. That means more deaths, more destruction. And even that won't be the end. In their mutual competition both superpowers just keep building more. More madness. More suicide. More idolatry.

They aren't superpowers, they're superlemmings, headed for destruction. You know the story of the lemmings—those Scandinavian rodents who for some reason every few years go on a mass migration and all rush together into the sea to their destruction. Do we look like superpowers or superlemmings?

In the most desperate way, we need repentance, we need guidance, we need hope, we need deliverance from our fears and our hates, deliverance into love and joy and peace. Is there a space age Noah's ark? Is there a time machine for escape? Is the Sermon on the Mount our time machine, a way given by Christ for us, so we can avoid the destruction and desolation of nuclear war?

We may have missed the guidance offered by the Sermon on the Mount because we have read it only as a teaching about *not* doing something—turn the other cheek, don't hit back. We argue whether a Christian should ever fight in wartime. Some argue no, and point to the injustice of the

Vietnam war. Others argue yes, and point to a relatively just war like World War II. And then neither does much about positive peacemaking.

That argument misses much of the point. Jesus is emphasizing not simply what we *shouldn't* do, but what we *should* do, actively. Howard Rees used to ask: "What I want to know, is what *are* you doing while you're not doing what you don't do?"

The Sermon on the Mount maps out the positive action that we desperately need to begin doing. May this positive action be the way of survival rather than destruction? What are Jesus' positive steps of peacemaking?

1. *Take imaginative, surprising, empathetic initiative.* Jesus says, "Happy are the peacemakers." The word "peacemakers" doesn't simply mean don't do violence, or don't make war. It means use your imagination, figure out ways you can take active initiative, surprising initiative, to make peace. And then you'll have hope; you'll be sons of God.

2. *Go talk to your brother.* Jesus says if you are coming to church to worship, and there remember that your brother has something against you, drop your hymnbook right there, and run, get reconciled to your brother, and only then come back and sing your hymn. Jesus really means this. This is how I am to deal with someone who has something against me, or with someone whom I have something against. Don't build up resentment. Don't spread rumors. Don't dream of revenge. Don't talk to somebody else about it. Go straight to your brother and talk to him. Explain it to him. Work out a reconciliation. Enmity means wanting to say, "I'm sorry."

3. *Go two miles to make peace.* Jesus says don't take vengeance, but if any one forces you to go with him one mile, go with him two miles. In his day it was the Zealots who advocated armed rebellion against the oppressive Roman government; they wanted vengeance for all their injustice. Every year, someone would try to start an insurrection against the Roman centurions, and would be put to death by the Romans. It was guerrilla war. And it

finally erupted into full-scale war, and the Jews lost, and the Romans tore down the city wall, and destroyed the Temple, and scattered the Jews so they could not return until the twentieth century. The bitterness of that tragedy is still the climactic part of present-day Jewish weddings, and its consequences still threaten to erupt into war in the Mideast.

Jesus took a direct stand against the Zealot political strategy. In his day a Roman centurion had authority to order a Jew to carry his pack one mile. The Zealots advocated violent resistance. Jesus said we should surprise them and carry the packs two miles. Take surprising initiative; make peace with the hated Roman enemy.

Jesus was taking a stand on the most controversial political issue of peace and war of his day. Some people misinterpret the Sermon on the Mount so that it applies only to peace of mind or to individual relations and does not get involved in political issues. But doesn't that limit Jesus' lordship? Jesus is Lord of all of life. Jesus took a stand on the most controversial political issue of his day. He advocated an alternative strategy which is beautifully symbolized by his inclusion of a Zealot, Simon, and a tax collector, Matthew-Levi, in the band of disciples. "Love your enemies" was not merely an ideal, it was a daily practice of the early Christian community.

4. *Feed the hungry, aid the poor.* Jesus says don't covet economic possessions, but give to him who begs. One of the biggest causes of war is the greed of those who have, and the hunger of those who have not. War is caused by injustice. We can take our part in making peace by giving to combat world hunger. We can form a group to study the causes of world hunger. We can drastically cut our consumption of gasoline, because demand for oil causes worldwide oil price inflation, and makes hungry nations unable to afford fertilizer and investment in food production. We can support the push for human rights, for justice around the world. Injustice causes war.

5. *Don't call your brother fool; respect him.* Jesus says

don't kill, don't stew in anger, don't put down your brother and call him fool. He says this because he has an alternate way, a way to be reconciled: Respect your brother; go talk with him. In a world where we can exterminate one another, the future has to be built on mutual respect.

But how can you talk to the Russians? They've got all these bombs, and they violate human rights, and they invade Afghanistan and cruelly kill their independence. True, but they share one interest with us: they don't want to get bombed either. The nuclear arms race has put us both in the same boat, on the same fragile earth, potential victims of the very same idolatrous way of destruction.

We can talk about ways to slow the nuclear arms race—ways that can be monitored by our own scientific satellites and infrared cameras and radio and microwave interceptors—so that we know what they're building, and whether they're keeping the agreements. That's why the Southern Baptist Convention, meeting in Houston last summer, called on all of us to support the SALT II treaty as a minimal step toward real reductions, and to write our Senators urging them to support the way of mutual reduction of these weapons on both sides. And called on all of us to pray for peace, and to preach and teach peace in our churches.

6. *Pray for your enemies.* Jesus says, "Love your enemies and pray for those who persecute you." Peacemaking is not only the outward actions you take; it is inward, too. It is prayer. Because war is first made in the human heart. We have anger bottled up inside us. We have self-righteousness and blame bottled up. We have idolatrous nationalism inside us. We see the speck in their eye but miss the log in our own eye. We need to pray, deeply and sincerely, for our enemies.

I have a practical suggestion: In our churches, it is our custom to pray regularly for those who are sick. Why can't we also pray regularly for those who are the victims of war? In Ireland and Iran, in Zimbabwe—Rhodesia, and Cambodia, and right here and in Russia when major nuclear war comes—that will be sickness in doses we have never seen or even thought of.

"Love your enemies." I love my family. I have three teen-age boys—Michael, Bill, David—and my wife, Dot. I have gotten my love involved in my wife and in my three sons, and I believe the odds are strong they will feel the awful destruction of nuclear war. And your children, too, and parents and brothers and sisters, too. And Russian children, too. Russians have families and children whom they love, as I love my family. Love the Russian children. Pray for them regularly. Be ye merciful, even as your Father in heaven is merciful.

How is the Sermon on the Mount a way to survive the future? It gives us six practical steps of peacemaking:

Take imaginative, surprising empathetic initiative.

Go talk to your brother.

Go two miles to make peace.

Feed the hungry, aid the poor.

Don't call your brother fool; respect him.

Pray for your enemies.

The Sermon on the Mount is a promise of participation in God's love, in God's Kingdom, in God's deliverance, now as we repent and become peacemakers, and eternally in fellowship with him. Peacemakers are blessed, for they are sons of God. This helps us face the reality of our fears.

The Sermon on the Mount may enable us to repent enough and take these six practical steps of peacemaking and avoid major nuclear war. I hope so. I pray so. But it will take more than complacency and inactivity.

And if we fail, if we do not avoid major nuclear war, the Sermon on the Mount in us may begin to grow a people, the Elois, or the Christians, a remnant of whom will do better as peacemaking people after the destruction, the second time around.

I have not told you the ending of the TV movie "The Time Machine." The scientist joins the Elois—the remnant of humanity—hoping humanity can start *again,* but this time in peace. The Time Machine becomes a symbol of hope *after* destruction.

In the Sermon on the Mount, Jesus is offering us hope and a challenge: to follow him; to follow his teachings; to be peace*makers* who will be called sons of God. To do better in *this* time; and if necessary, to plant the seeds for the remnant that will do better the second time around.

NOTES

1. Available from Sojourners, 1309 L. Street, NW, Washington, DC 20005.
2. *The Military Balance,* 1979–1980, International Institute of Strategic Studies (London: 1979), pp. 3-4.
3. Extrapolation from studies by Congressman Les Aspin, Paul Nitze, and Glen Stassen.

WILLIAM D. THOMPSON

The Wherever God

Psalm 139

I recently talked with a patient in a hospital for emotionally disturbed people. We sat in the dayroom, enjoying as much privacy as you can in a place like that. I asked her why she kept glancing around, and she said that, even though she knew the videotape cameras were in special, smaller rooms, wherever she was she felt the cold stare of those video cameras. "Just like God, always looking at you," she said.

And I thought of the psalmist who in a place far from here and a time long ago felt the presence of God—not the presence of a cold camera's stare but the warm presence of a person with an arm outstretched, pointing the way, and a right hand to steady.

It was not that he wanted to flee from God's presence that he wrote, "Whither shall I go from thy spirit? or whither shall I flee from thy presence?" It was a rhetorical question. Or was it? Was there some urge deep within him—a thought that gave birth to the words that produced a flight away from the God he wrote the song to praise? We know because we flee from this presence with regularity.

To us the flight from God's presence may really be our avoidance of a God who is trying to say something to us. We have heard about the ways we are likely to flee from God's presence into our liquor or sex or Eastern religions or even the boob tube. Our being here puts us in touch with the God we should and want to hear—really want to hear—but whose channels of communication we may have shut off, sometimes with no intention at all to do so.

Neither this psalmist nor any biblical writer has prepared a list of God's channels of communication. The natural variety of the psalmist's experiences with God produces the beginning of the list and nudges our memories with stories from Eden to Patmos where God has sought—and sometimes found—a way to communicate himself. He got through to Elijah not in the wind or fire or earthquake but in the still, small voice. A cross was God's way once. At Pentecost he did come in the wind, and on the road to Damascus in a blinding light and a fall to earth.

The problem in our communication with God is not his lack of channels or his skill in using them but in our need to limit those channels. That woman in the mental hospital is ready to go home—her insight sharpened and her temper tamed. But she is not sure that she wants to. The hospital routine, the finely tuned relationships with staff, and the safe environment make the prospect of going home pretty scary. We know what that is like and we act like that. We eat the same kind of meat, drive the same route home, vacation in the same cottage, and read the same magazines all the time where we feel safe and life is predictable. We say the same thing in every prayer, respond in conversation with the same safe, pat phrases, and give our attention to the same few people—the ones who like us and stroke us. Have you noticed how common the words have become in the last couple of years—"I'm not comfortable doing it that way" or "Are you comfortable with that idea?" The channels in which we communicate are familiar, comfortable. We live in a kind of comfort zone whose borders we violate at our peril. And woe to the God who tries to get in.

Perhaps worse than any of that is that we try to find God on a channel that he is not even on. In the events leading to the cross, Jesus' followers had the dial on a political channel. Brother Lawrence sought God at the altar, but God was in the kitchen—in the pots and pans. Jeb

Magruder tuned in to the White House for important information, but he found it in Jesus Christ, in the front seat of a car, and in conversation with a pastor.

Why is it that we think we determine how God will communicate with us—that he comes only in the quiet time or the sermon or a devotional booklet? Why is it that we think he speaks to us only of "spiritual" things and not of how we vote or where we throw our Big Mac wrappers or how we determine the size of our family? Maybe we think that he is not going to say anything we have not already heard—the last important bit of information picked up in the junior-high department of the Sunday school or even in the last issue of the denominational journal. Or maybe we fear that he will say something we have already heard and done nothing about. We close our ears and shut out the channel, going from his spirit and fleeing from his presence.

And that sermon, that quiet time—maybe God is not there at all for you today. Maybe his voice is coming from the derelict on the subway steps, the bizarre behavior of some McMurphy who brings caring and redeeming love into a cuckoo's nest, or an assistant personnel director who confers with two feuding workers on the assembly line and sends them back with their arms around each other. Maybe his voice comes from an obese black nurse's aide with strong, tender arms and the promise of a prayer.

Whatever else we know of God, we know that he is everywhere trying to communicate with us. If I ascend up into heaven, thou art there: if I make my bed in Sheol, behold, thou art there. If I take the wings of the morning and dwell in the uttermost parts of the sea: even there shall thy hand lead me, and thy right hand shall hold me" (KJV).

I do not know what God may be wanting to say to you, except in a very general way, or how he may be wanting to say it. I do know how he has spoken to me and to men and women like you who have shaped the community I live in and who have shared with me their experiences of God. I know that sometimes he speaks around a table in the seminary coffee shop through a visitor to our campus who has walked with him through body-littered streets in India. Or to a commuting student who gave death the slip on a rain-battered I-95. I have heard him in a provocative lecture by a skilled scholar and in a half-sentence of penetrating insight in another lecture from whose dullness I had yearned only a few minutes before to be delivered. God has spoken in a muscially inferior gospel chorus badly sung on the radio on a lonely drive. It has got to be God in the kiss of a four-year-old after I have preached a halting children's sermon on the chancel steps. And who else is it but God in the spouse who listens patiently about the impossible demands of a stupid, neurotic boss and who lovingly lets you cry or withdraw or blast the pictures off the wall? Is it not God who reveals himself in the cool, spring air and in the stark beauty of the monochrome painting on the wall behind the branch manager at the bank, and in the newscast that a state mediator has settled the teachers' strike in your town, and in the Gideon Bible you pick up in the motel whose words make you say, "Aha"? "If I take the wings of the morning, and dwell in the uttermost parts of the sea, behold"—you are trying to break through my shortsightedness, the limited repertoire of communication channels I think you use. "Thou hast beset me behind and before, and laid thine hand upon me."

He speaks . . . wherever . . . whenever . . . however. To him be honor and praise, glory and blessing, now and always. Amen.

PAUL TILLICH

You Are Accepted

*Moreover the law entered, that the offence might
abound. But where sin abounded, grace did much
more abound.*

—Romans 5:20 KJV

These words of Paul summarize his apostolic experience,
his religious message as a whole, and the Christian
understanding of life. To discuss these words, or to make
them the text of even several sermons, has always seemed
impossible to me. I have never dared to use them before.
But something has driven me to consider them during the
past few months, a desire to give witness to the two facts
which appeared to me, in hours of retrospection, as the
all-determining facts of our life: the abounding of sin and
the greater abounding of grace.

There are few words more strange to most of us than
"sin" and "grace." They are strange, just because they are
so well-known. During the centuries they have received
distorting connotations, and have lost so much of their
genuine power that we must seriously ask ourselves
whether we should use them at all, or whether we should
discard them as useless tools. But there is a mysterious
fact about the great words of our religious tradition: they
cannot be replaced. All attempts to make substitutions,
including those I have tried myself, have failed to convey
the reality that was to be expressed; they have led to

shallow and impotent talk. There are no substitutes for words like "sin" and "grace." But there *is* a way of rediscovering their meaning, the same way that leads us down into the depth of our human existence. In that depth these words were conceived; and *there* they gained power for all ages; *there* they must be found again by each generation, and by each of us for himself. Let us therefore try to penetrate the deeper levels of our life, in order to see whether we can discover in them the realities of which our text speaks.

Have the men of our time still a feeling of the meaning of sin? Do they, and do we, still realize that sin does *not* mean an immoral act, that "sin" should never be used in the plural, and that not our sins, but rather our *sin* is the great, all-pervading problem of our life? Do we still know that it is arrogant and erroneous to divide men by calling some "sinners" and others "righteous"? For by way of such a division, we can usually discover that we ourselves do not *quite* belong to the "sinners," since we have avoided heavy sins, have made some progress in the control of this or that sin, and have been even humble enough not to call ourselves "righteous." Are we still able to realize that this kind of thinking and feeling about sin is far removed from what the great religious tradition, both within and outside the Bible, has meant when it speaks of sin?

I should like to suggest another word to you, not as a substitute for the word "sin," but as a useful clue in the interpretation of the word "sin": "separation." Separation is an aspect of the experience of everyone. Perhaps the word "sin" has the same root as the word "asunder." In any case, *sin is separation.* To be in the state of sin is to be in the state of separation. And separation is threefold: there is separation among individual lives, separation of a man from himself, and separation of all men from the Ground of Being. This threefold separation constitutes the state of everything that exists; it is a universal fact; it is the fate of every life. And it is our human fate in a very special sense. For *we* as men know that we are separated. We not only suffer with all other creatures because of the self-destructive consequences of our separation, but also know *why* we suffer. We know that we are estranged from something to which we really belong, and with which we *should* be united. We know that the fate of separation is not merely a natural event like a flash of sudden lightning, but that it is an experience in which we actively participate, in which our whole personality is involved, and that, as fate, it is also *guilt*. Separation which is fate *and* guilt constitutes the meaning of the word "sin." It is *this* which is the state of our entire existence, from its very beginning to its very end. Such separation is prepared in the mother's womb, and before that time, in every preceding generation. It is manifest in the special actions of our conscious life. It reaches beyond our graves into all the succeeding generations. It is our existence itself. *Existence is separation!* Before sin is an act, it is a state.

We can say the same things about grace. For sin and grace are bound to each other. We do not even have a knowledge of sin unless we have already experienced the unity of life, which is grace. And conversely, we could not grasp the meaning of grace without having experienced the separation of life, which is sin. Grace is just as difficult to describe as sin. For some people, grace is the willingness of a divine king and father to forgive over and again the foolishness and weakness of his subjects and children. We must reject such a concept of grace; for it is a merely childish destruction of a human dignity. For others grace is a magic power in the dark places of the soul, but a power without any significance for practical life, a quickly vanishing and useless idea. For others, grace is the benevolence that we may find beside the cruelty and destructiveness in life. But then, it does not matter whether we say "life goes on," or whether we say "there is grace in life"; if grace means no more than this, the word should, and will, disappear. For other people, grace indicates the gifts that one has received from nature or society, and the power to do good things with the help of those gifts. But grace is more than gifts. In grace something is overcome; grace occurs "in spite of" something; grace occurs in spite of separation and estrangement. Grace is the *re*union of life with life, the *re*conciliation of the self with itself. Grace transforms fate into a meaningful destiny; it changes guilt into confidence and courage. There is something triumphant in the word "grace": in spite of the abounding of sin grace abounds much more.

And now let us look down into ourselves to discover there the struggle between separation and reunion, between sin and grace, in our relation to others, in our relation to ourselves, and in our relation to the Ground and aim of our being. If our souls respond to the description that I intend to give, words like "sin" and "separation," "grace" and "reunion," may have a new meaning for us. But the words themselves are not important. It is the response of the deepest levels of our being that is important. If such a response were to occur among us this moment, we could say that we have known grace.

Who has not, at some time, been lonely in the midst of a social event? The feeling of our separation from the rest of life is most acute when we are surrounded by it in noise and talk. We realize then much more than in moments of solitude how strange we are to one another, how estranged life is from life. Each one of us draws back into himself. We cannot penetrate the hidden center of another individual; nor can that individual pass beyond the shroud that covers our own being. Even the greatest love cannot break through the walls of the self. Who has not experienced that disillusionment of all great love? If one were to hurl away his self in complete self-surrender, he would become a nothing, without form or strength, a self without self, merely an object of contempt and abuse. Our generation knows more than the generation of our fathers about the hidden hostility in the ground of our souls. Today we know much about the profusive aggressiveness in every being. Today we can confirm what Immanuel Kant, the prophet of human reason and dignity, was honest enough to say: there is something in the misfortune of our best friends which does not displease us. Who among us is dishonest enough to deny that this is true also of him? Are we not almost always ready to abuse everybody and everything, although often in a very refined way, for the pleasure of self-elevation, for an occasion for boasting, for a moment of lust? To know that we are ready is to know the meaning of the separation of life from life, and of "sin abounding."

The most irrevocable expression of the separation of life from life today is the attitude of social groups within nations toward each other, and the attitude of nations themselves toward other nations. The walls of distance, in time and space, have been removed by technical progress; but the walls of estrangement between heart and heart have been incredibly strengthened. The madness of the German Nazis and the cruelty of the lynching mobs in the South provide too easy an excuse for us to turn our thoughts from our own selves. But let us just consider ourselves and what we feel, when we read, this morning and tonight, that in some sections of Europe all children under the age of three are sick and dying, or that in some sections of Asia millions without homes are freezing and starving to death. The strangeness of life to life is evident in the strange fact that we can know all this, and yet can live today, this morning, tonight, as though we were completely ignorant. And I refer to the most sensitive people among us. In both mankind and nature, life is separated from life. Estrangement prevails among all things that live. Sin abounds.

It is important to remember that we are not merely separated from one another. For we are also separated from ourselves. *Man Against Himself* is not merely the title of a book, but rather also indicates the rediscovery of an age-old insight. Man is split within himself. Life moves against itself through aggression, hate, and despair. We are wont to condemn self-love; but what we really mean to condemn is contrary to self-love. It is that mixture of selfishness and self-hate that permanently pursues us, that prevents us from loving others, and that prohibits us from losing ourselves in the love with which we are loved eternally. He who is able to love himself is able to love others also; he who has learned to overcome self-contempt has overcome his contempt for others. But the depth of our separation lies in just the fact that we are not capable of a great and merciful divine love toward ourselves. On the contrary, in each of us there is an instinct of self-destruction, which is as strong as our instinct of self-preservation. In our tendency to abuse and destroy others, there is an open or hidden tendency to abuse and to destroy ourselves. Cruelty toward others is always also cruelty toward ourselves. Nothing is more obvious than the split in both our unconscious life and conscious personality. Without the help of modern psychology, Paul expressed the fact in his famous words, "For I do not do the good I desire, but rather the evil that I do not desire." And then he continued in words that might well be the motto of all depth psychology: "Now if I should do what I do not wish to do, it is not I that do it, but rather sin which dwells within me." The apostle sensed a split between his conscious will and his real will, between himself and something strange within and alien to him. He was estranged from himself, and that estrangement he called "sin." He also called it a strange "law in his limbs," an irresistible compulsion. How often we commit certain acts in perfect consciousness, yet with the shocking sense that we are being controlled by an alien power! That is the experience of the separation of ourselves from ourselves, which is to say "sin," whether or not we like to use that word.

Thus, the state of our whole life is estrangement from others and ourselves, because we are estranged from the Ground of our being, because we are estranged from the origin and aim of our life. And we do not know where we have come from, or where we are going. We are separated from the mystery, the depth, and the greatness of our existence. We hear the voice of that depth; but our ears are closed. We feel that something radical, total, and unconditioned is demanded of us; but we rebel against it, try to escape its urgency, and will not accept its promise.

We cannot escape, however. If that something is the Ground of our being, we are bound to it for all eternity, just as we are bound to ourselves and to all other life. We always remain in the power of that from which we are estranged. That fact brings us to the ultimate depth of sin: separated and yet bound, estranged and yet belonging, destroyed and yet preserved, the state which is called despair. Despair means that there is no escape. Despair is "the sickness unto death." But the terrible thing about the sickness of despair is that we cannot be released, not even through open or hidden suicide. For we all know that we are bound eternally and inescapably to the Ground of our being. The abyss of separation is not always visible. But it has become more visible to our generation than to the preceding generations, because of our feeling of meaninglessness, emptiness, doubt, and cynicism—all expressions of despair, of our separation from the roots and the meaning of our life. Sin in its most profound sense, sin, as despair, abounds among us.

"Where sin abounded, grace did much more abound," says Paul in the same letter in which he describes the unimaginable power of separation and self-destruction within society and the individual soul. He does not say these words because sentimental interests demand a happy ending for everything tragic. He says them because they describe the most overwhelming and determining experience of his life. In the picture of Jesus as the Christ, which appeared to him at the moment of his greatest separation from other men, from himself and God, he found himself accepted in spite of his being rejected. And when he found that he was accepted, he was able to accept himself and to be reconciled to others. The moment in which grace struck him and overwhelmed him, he was reunited with that to which he belonged, and from which he was estranged in utter strangeness. Do we know what it means to be struck by grace? It does *not* mean that we suddenly believe that God exists, or that Jesus is the Savior, or that the Bible contains the truth. To believe that something *is,* is almost contrary to the meaning of grace. Furthermore, grace does not mean simply that we are making progress in our moral self-control, in our fight against special faults, and in our relationships to men and to society. Moral progress may be a fruit of grace; but it is not grace itself, and it can even prevent us from receiving grace. For there is too often a graceless acceptance of Christian doctrines and a graceless battle against the structures of evil in our personalities. Such a graceless relation to God may lead us by necessity either to arrogance or to despair. It would be better to refuse God and the Christ and the Bible than to accept Them without grace. For if we accept without grace, we do so in the state of separation, and can only succeed in deepening the separation. We cannot transform our lives, unless we allow them to be transformed by that stroke of grace. It happens; or it does not happen. And certainly it does *not* happen if we try to force it upon ourselves, just as it shall not happen so long as we think, in our self-complacency, that we have no need of it. Grace strikes us when we are in great pain and restlessness. It strikes us when we walk through the dark valley of a meaningless and empty life. It strikes us when we feel that our separation is deeper than usual, because we have violated another life, a life which we loved, or from which we were estranged. It strikes us when our disgust for our own being, our indifference, our weakness, our hostility, and our lack of direction and composure have become intolerable to us. It strikes us when, year after year, the longed-for perfection of life does not appear, when the old compulsions reign within us as they have for decades, when despair destroys all joy and courage. Sometimes at that moment a wave of light breaks into our darkness, and it is as though a voice were saying: "You are accepted. *You are accepted,* accepted by that which is greater than you, and the name of which you do not know. Do not ask for the name now; perhaps you will find it later. Do not try to do anything now; perhaps later you will do much. Do not seek for anything; do not perform anything; do not intend anything. *Simply accept the fact that you are accepted!"* If that happens to us, we experience grace. After such an experience we may not be better than before, and we may not believe more than before. But everything is transformed. In that moment, grace conquers sin, and reconciliation bridges the gulf of estrangement. And nothing is demanded of this experience, no religious or moral or intellectual presupposition, nothing but *acceptance*.

In the light of this grace we perceive the power of grace in our relation to others and to ourselves. We experience the grace of being able to look frankly into the eyes of another, the miraculous grace of reunion of life with life. We experience the grace of understanding one another's words. We understand not merely the literal meaning of the words, but also that which lies behind them, even when they are harsh or angry. For even then there is a longing to break through the walls of separation. We experience the grace of being able to accept the life of another, even if it be hostile and harmful to us, for, through grace, we know that it belongs to the same Ground to which we belong, and by which we have been accepted. We experience the grace which is able to overcome the tragic separation of the sexes, of the generations, of the nations, of the races, and even the utter strangeness between man and nature. Sometimes grace appears in all these separations to reunite us with those to whom we belong. For life belongs to life.

And in the light of this grace we perceive the power of grace in our relation to ourselves. We experience moments in which we accept ourselves, because we feel that we have been accepted by that which is greater than we. If only more such moments were given to us! For it is such moments that make us love our life, that make us accept ourselves not in our goodness and self-complacency, but in our certainty of the eternal meaning of our life. We cannot force ourselves to accept ourselves. We cannot compel anyone to accept himself. But sometimes it happens that we receive the power to say yes to ourselves, that peace enters into us and makes us whole, that self-hate and self-contempt disappear, and that our self is reunited with itself. Then we can say that grace has come upon us.

"Sin" and "grace" are strange words, but they are not strange things. We find them whenever we look into ourselves with searching eyes and longing hearts. They determine our life. They abound within us and in all of life. May grace more abound within us!

K. H. TING

"Give Ye Them to Eat"

Luke 9:12-17

In the wonderful story of the feeding of the five thousand, there are a few things to which I wish to call your attention. First, the disciples thought that Christ's work consisted only of *talking* about the Kingdom. As to the matter of feeding the multitude, it was none of his business, and therefore none of their business either. They said, send the crowd away; let them all go their own ways and obtain whatever food they can. But Christ said, give ye them to eat.

Now, what the disciples were advocating was actually the principle of looking out for oneself—that is, each person doing his or her own thing. If this principle is put into practice, as indeed it once was in China and has been elsewhere, the result is inevitably for the strong and mighty to dominate and for the common people to be their victims. It all ends up in a full-fledged capitalism, which is defined by John Maynard Keynes as "the extraordinary belief that the nastiest of men for the nastiest of motives will somehow work for the benefit of us all." Of course, we know that it doesn't work out that way.

Second, in order to feed the people, Christ instructed the disciples that the multitude be divided into groups of roughly fifty people each and that they all be seated in those groups rather than walking about in disorder. Since it was Christ who gave these instructions, perhaps people would be kind enough not to term them regimentation or curtailment of individual freedom. They constituted, let us say, a certain discouragement of individualism, a certain amount of program-planning and organization. We know from our experience in China that such organization is necessary.

I

Let us note also that Christ looked up to heaven, blessed the food and broke the bread, giving it to the disciples to set before the multitude. My guess is that there were many views and shades of opinion among those people concerning the person of Jesus Christ. And Christ respected them all. His care was for the whole multitude, indeed for all of humanity, not just for those who knew him personally. God is so great that it would be contrary to his nature for his love and care to be reserved only for those who consciously profess his name. I don't think he minds terribly that there are those who for some reason or other cannot acknowledge him and feel constrained to deny his existence.

Still another consideration is the fact that, although the occasion was far from being a banquet, there was no shortage of food. Everyone could be satisfied. No one needed to suffer from starvation. What relief it must be for parents to know their children won't need to go to bed at night in hunger. And that is an important part of the meaning of the word liberation. When I say that China is a liberated country, I have in mind the fact that, through planning and organization, we are able to feed almost one-fourth of humanity with the food produced on only one-seventh of the earth's arable land. This is not a miracle as Christ's was, but it is an achievement for which we want to thank God.

Let us note further that though twelve basketfuls of food were left over, nothing is said about what happened to them. Where did they go? Were they thrown in the garbage? Just left on the scene to be devoured by animals?

Sold to someone who could pay a good price and who hoarded the food until a shortage forced the market price up and he could profit—making the rich still richer and the poor still poorer? The biblical silence on the disposal of the leftover food sets us thinking. Usually the Christian message comes to us in what the Bible says, but sometimes it comes in what the Bible refrains from saying. Here is a guiding principle for Bible study: sometimes there is a still small voice in biblical silence.

Is it possible that the silence of Luke's Gospel on this very point is intended so that the Holy Spirit can lead us into seeing that the problem was not really solved by feeding five thousand people once? What can twelve basketfuls of food do to relieve the hunger of fifty thousand, or five hundred thousand, or the five and even fifty million poor people of the world? So this biblical silence becomes for us a symbol of the unfinished responsibility, a symbol of the unhelpfulness of mere philanthropy in a world in which poverty and hunger are mounting at a much faster rate than our kindhearted philanthropists can cope with. Traditional ethics looks only at the individuals—the hungry people on the street, the beggars, the thieves and the robbers—but the mystery of the twelve basketfuls urges us to examine the entire social order.

II

Our good earth can produce enough for everybody's need, but it cannot produce enough for everybody's greed. How are we to distribute wealth and opportunities more justly and fairly? That is the question the gospel story raises for us.

When I was a primary school boy, I lived in Shanghai. I knew something of how the wealthy lived in those days. But some miles away was Yangchow, an area so poor that whenever a drought occurred—and that was often—men and women from Yangchow would come to Shanghai barefoot and in rags, in groups big and small, to seek work. They were so bony and lifeless that their very appearance was frightening to me. They didn't really expect any wages; they would work just for food in order to survive, But many could find neither work nor food. They became beggars. Some of them died on the street because of hunger or cold. Girls were bought to be prostitutes. For boys, to be accepted as an apprentice in a barber shop and eventually to become a barber would be considered the best of luck. These downtrodden souls constituted the majority of our people.

Some two years ago I visited that area again. No longer are there landlords to extort exorbitant rentals from the peasants. There is hydraulic irrigation now. People are living in brick houses rather than mud ones. Men and women are studying, from kindergarten to university, or are working in a factory or on a farm. Many women factory workers wear leather shoes and wristwatches. Some of them wear woolen trousers and Dacron shirts, with a pen or two in the pocket. And they have bikes, too. These things may not mean much to you, but to them it constitutes a tremendous change. When I heard their laughter, I was almost in tears, because I was thinking of the plight of their forebears. How I wished to tell the young people there of what I had seen in the past so that they wouldn't forget.

There are defects, mistakes and excesses in China; it is not a paradise. But certainly it now has much more equitable distribution of wealth and opportunities. The landlords have become working people, too. All of this has been brought about through a great social upheaval, the ownership of the means of production having been changed from a small section of our population to the masses of the people themselves. We call that liberation. It is liberation in the true sense of the word because our people have gained freedom, not lost it, and are now able to work through organized efforts for greater freedom for themselves and for future generations.

III

Christians do have good reasons to be concerned with the question of material distribution. After his resurrection,

Christ walked with two of his disciples on their way to Emmaus. It was not when he was expounding the Scriptures to them that they came to know who he was. Nor was it when he sat down to eat with them. It was only when he took bread, blessed it and gave it to them that their eyes were opened and they knew him to be the Christ. So could we not say that the equitable distribution of bread to humanity really has something of the sacrament in it? The way wealth and opportunities are distributed—i.e., the way society is organized—has a lot to do with the manifestation of Jesus Christ to men and women. We know that the God whom Jesus Christ came to reveal to us is a God who is at the same time loving and almighty. This sort of God is really not easy to conceive of. For people who have experienced injustice, deprivation, and suffering, for whom nothing in life is cheerful or joyous, it is much easier to conceive of a God who is loving but not almighty, or a God who is almighty but not loving, or a God who is neither.

And yet we insist that God is both loving and almighty despite the evils and suffering around us. To believe this demands a lot from people. So it is not surprising that many want to abandon the Christian conception of God—or that they feel attracted to the death-of-God hypothesis. The death of God as a theological fad was brief indeed, but the death of God as a philosophy of the conduct of life is spreading. Writes Richard L. Rubenstein: "When I say we live in the time of the death of God, I mean that the thread uniting God and humanity, heaven and earth, has been broken. We stand in a cold, silent unfeeling cosmos, unaided by any purposeful power beyond our own resources. After Auschwitz, what else can a Jew say about God?"

So here in a clear-cut way, we see how social, economic and political injustice eats away at people's faith in a God who is at once almighty and loving. Only the achievement of a healthier social system and a fairer distribution of the world's goods, with all the prosperity, peace, joy, and progress such distribution entails, will enable men and women to see reasonableness in the Christian conception of God—the God who is the Father Almighty—and to find cause for thanksgiving to that God. Thus the question of distribution has a very important evangelistic dimension—a dimension which we must not lose sight of. Though the water which runs through the hydraulic irrigation system in Yangchow is cold, I like to think of the warmth it brings to human life—the warmth in the hearts of parents who today can give full rice bowls to their children, the warmth of the assurance that their adolescent daughters will not be compelled by hunger to do anything unworthy of self-respect.

Matter, in my view, is not in itself evil; it has been made into a channel for transmitting the grace of God. This is sacrament in the rudimentary sense of the word, for matter can represent and convey something of God's love and care to men and women.

Let us be serious when we say that this is God's world. If it is God's, it cannot be Satan's. The thread uniting God and humanity, heaven and earth, has not been broken, and we do not stand in a cold, silent, unfeeling cosmos. God the Father Almighty, the all-loving and all-powerful God, God the Creator, is today carrying on his work of creation to its completion. What we human beings do with our hands and minds is meaningful, is of value, is not to be destroyed or thrown out at the end of history, but is to be received into the hand of God, is to be sublimated, to be transfigured, to be perfected. As Thomas Aquinas said, grace does not supplant nature; rather, it perfects nature. For the incarnation of the son of God to have happened at all means that there is not a total disparity between God and the world, between grace and nature. To say that humankind is fallen is to say that people are not now in their proper state, the state in which they belong, the state for which they are intended. It certainly does not mean that all their work is for nothing.

IV

Recall the words of Paul in Romans 5: "If by the offense of the one man all died, much more"—let's emphasize "much more"—"did the grace of God and the gracious gift of the one man Jesus Christ abound for all." In other words, we are born not only in original sin but also, and much more so, in original grace. The incarnation of the son of God has surely made more of an impact on humanity than the fall of Adam. Human solidarity with Christ is more universal, more powerful, than human solidarity with Adam through sin. We believe in a universality of divine grace. We look at the world in the splendor of the ascended Christ. What human beings do to promote community, to make love more possible and more available to people, is consonant with God's work of creation, because God himself—the Father, Son, and Holy Spirit—has the image of the loving community; humanity was created in that image and is moving in the direction of recovering that image. This how we look at the world and at history, and at human aspirations, movements and struggles. It is a source of our optimism and thanksgiving.

The German writer Bertolt Brecht had this to say about the humanly unlivable society in which he found himself:

> Those who take the meat from the table
> Teach contentment.
> Those for whom the taxes are destined
> Demand sacrifice.
> Those who eat their fill speak to the hungry
> Of the wonderful time to come.
> Those who lead the country into the abyss
> Call ruling too difficult
> For ordinary folk.

The feeding of the five thousand takes us to an entirely different world—a world which is a community of sharing, a world in which life is organized so that men and women can be brothers and sisters to each other. As we live our daily life, may the vision of this coming world sustain us in the fellowship of faith, love and hope.

WILLIAM P. TUCK

Exorcising Demons in the Modern World

Mark 5:1-20

The eyes of the demonic seem to be burning brighter again with the appearance of movies and novels like *Rosemary's Baby* and *The Exorcist*. Although the world is in a scientific and technological revolution, the impact of the occult with its astrology, seances, Satan cults, witches, horoscopes, and drugs reveals an emerging force which must be confronted in the Age of Aquarius. In this sense, then, the story of Jesus and the demoniac from the fifth chapter of Mark's Gospel, while sounding a bit like a tale of Edgar Allan Poe, does have a faint contemporary ring.

The disciples never forgot the experience with the demoniac of Gadara. So vivid was it in their minds that all three of the Synoptic Gospels record it. After an exhausting day Jesus and his disciples took a small boat across the Sea of Galilee. The tiny craft was caught in a sudden storm whose fury became so intense that it lashed fear into all the disciples, even the experienced fishermen. The strained nerves of the disciples found strength in the words from Christ, "Peace, be still." As suddenly as it had arisen, the storm subsided. But the stillness of this peace was short-lived. A fury as wild and uncontrollable as the wind and the sea was to confront them.

As soon as the vessel touched the southern shore of the Sea of Galilee, Jesus and his disciples, with their nerves already on edge, began to climb slowly up the weird steep gorge to the bluff above. Suddenly out of the darkness of the mountain graveyard leaped a screaming, naked, hideous creature dragging and clanging the chains which were supposed to restrain him. His eyes were wide with derangement, his body was covered with huge bloody welts, his arms were waving wildly, his long hair was entangled in a mass of twisted knots, and his movement seemed to indicate that he possessed superhuman strength. With hair standing on end, knees knocking, cold shivers running up and down their spines, and their eyes bulging, the disciples must have been terrified at this breathtaking collision.

While the disciples were frozen with fear, the tormented creature threw himself at the feet of Jesus. With quiet confidence and the serene assurance of a man who seemed always ready for such an emergency, Jesus responded to the man's need instead of allowing appearances to frighten him so he could not act. Jesus the Master of the unexpected had already been saying to the man: "Come out of him, evil spirit." In Jesus' words to the demoniac the tense is important. From the moment of his encounter with the demoniac, Jesus had repeatedly ordered the demons to be exorcised, but his first efforts were unsuccessful. Then Jesus asked what might sound like a strange inquiry to us, "What is your name?" You might think, what importance could that possibly have? In an age when the belief in demon possession was prevalent, the knowledge of a demon's name gave the exorcists power over him. Instead of giving his name the demons replied with a number. We are six thousand. This was the number of soldiers in a Roman regiment. There are many of us; we are a mob; we are Legion.

The herd of swine on the slopes nearby indicated that Jesus and his disciples were in pagan country. No Jewish man would raise pigs. They were considered religiously unclean animals. The strange request by Legion to enter the hogs, if the demons were to be cheated out of a human habitat, was an attempt to avoid the abyss of the deep sea waters, where it was commonly held in biblical times was the final area of destruction for all evil spirits. Ironically, the force of the demonic entrance into the pigs was severe enough to send the whole herd of two thousand plunging dramatically to their deaths off the precipice into the depths of the sea.

Notice the epilogue. When the pig herdsmen rushed into the city and brought back the owners, did they rejoice at the great miracle which they had seen? They saw the demoniac sane, clothed, calm and talking normally with Jesus. Instead of celebrating in the wonder of the redemption which the demoniac received, the people feared Jesus, the exorcist, and asked him to leave. The demoniac was alone in expressing gratitude and asked Jesus to let him go with him. But Jesus sent him home and urged him to tell his friends about the power of God's gift of healing.

Now what are we to make of such a story today? Do we merely reject it as an ancient folk tale, reflecting the superstition and demonology of its time, with notions of magic and the occult? Some approach the problem of demonology as an ancient way of expressing what is called in contemporary society by psychiatric nomenclature. Biblical references to demon possession are seen as ancient descriptions of epilepsy, schizophrenia, or various forms of insanity. Without question there is much truth in this approach. Jesus himself did not attribute all illness to demon possession. The blind man, Jairus' daughter, the woman with the hemorrhage, the paralytic, and the centurion's servant, were all cases where Jesus did not associate these diseases with evil spirits. In some instances the healings of Jesus are clearly evidence that the person was either an epileptic or suffered from some kind of psychological disturbance. But the problem of demon possession in the New Testament cannot be solved that easily. It is apparent from a reading of the Gospels that Jesus not only spoke about the power of demons, he also exorcised them and commanded his disciples to cast them out in his name. Though it may seem embarrassing to a church which feels it has "come of age" and functions in a scientific age, the power to cast out demons was central to the ministry of Jesus. Harvey Cox noted this attitude when he declared that "most of us would prefer to forget that for many of his contemporaries Jesus' exorcism was in no way peripheral, but stood at the heart of his work."[1] The late Paul Tillich, in an address to the graduating students at Union Theological Seminary, affirmed that preaching Christ as the power to conquer the demonic forces that control our lives, mind and body, will prove to be the most adequate way to communicate the message of Christ for the people of our time.[2]

Can this possibly be true? How can this demonic imagery be meaningful to us today? *The answer lies in breaking through the prescientific images of demons and evil spirits to the reality to which they attest.* The New Testament acknowledges vividly the awesome power of evil in such images as "principalities and powers," "messengers of Satan," "rulers of darkness," "Satan, the father of lies and deception," "the Anti-Christ," "the Evil One," "the Adversary" and "the Destroyer." "Principalities and powers," a phrase that recurs frequently in the writings of Paul, was a common New Testament conception of the cosmic dimension of the power of evil.

Modern persons like to laugh at the old Cornish prayer: "From Ghoulies and Ghosties, and long-leggity Beasties, and all things that go bump in the night, Good Lord deliver us." We assert ourselves as too modern for that. We prefer "From systems, and ologies and isms, Good Lord free us." Evil becomes more comfortable for us when it is abstract and impersonal. Challenging this comfortable approach, Colin Morris, in a recent book, has stated: "I make no apology for calling evil by that old-fashioned, personal name, the Devil. It is a good way of keeping us alert to the fact there is about the operation of evil the subtlety of a malevolent personality rather than the crudity of a blind, irrational force."[3]

You do not think evil is real? Can we possibly believe that the depths and the dimensions of the Kingdom of Evil in the world are merely illusions of the mind? Tell the relatives of the six million Jews who were annihilated by the Nazis that there is no evidence of demonic power in the world. Tell the onlooking villagers at Mai Lai as they are staggered by the mountain of bodies of civilian men, women, and children that evil is an illusion. Tell the thousands of children fathered by American soldiers and deserted in Vietnam that there is no evidence of the power of evil. Is a child born blind because of syphilis from a prostitute not an argument for demonic power? Tell Sam Jones, who lost his left leg in Korea, that evil is abstract. Tell Mrs. Rush, who lost her son in Vietnam, that evil has no personal demonic dimension to it. Tell it to the parents whose son jumped from the twelfth story after an overdose of LSD. Are we really so civilized that we cannot see the awesome power of evil? We no longer throw ink wells at the devil as Martin Luther once did. We are too civilized for that, too mature! Yet one of the most civilized nations in the world exterminated six million human beings of one race. Let us be honest and admit it openly and forcefully as did the early New Testament Christians: evil is real and it is demonic. Somewhere we have lost the New Testament urgency of the unseen warfare. Without hesitation the New Testament senses a mighty contradiction at the heart of the universe. The New Testament writers pictured the Christian engaged in a combat with the forces of evil; but they shouted a ringing affirmation that in Jesus Christ, God has unleashed victory over sin, death, and the principalities and the powers.

Almost without exception the commentaries which I examined indicated that the demoniac passage was clearly one without any realistic theological or moral value for modern man. Without question, to my mind, this man Legion, the demoniac, rather than being out of focus for today's man, is symbolic of modern man. He is contemporary man, come of age. He is each of us. Legion refuses to allow us to be mere spectators in this story. We are participants. The demoniac becomes our mirror.

Jesus says, "What is your name?" "My name is Legion." I am many; I am a mob. I do not know who I am. There are many selves within me, and I am torn and pulled in every direction, seeking to find myself. How often we say, "I don't feel like myself today"; "I was nearly out of my mind"; "I said to myself—pull yourself together"; "Excuse my action, I just was not myself the other day"; "I am ashamed of myself"; "I forgot myself for the moment"; "I just hate myself for doing that." Each of us is rarely a unity; he or she is constantly at civil war within. In Arthur Miller's play *The Death of a Salesman,* the younger son, Biff, stands by his father's grave and reflects: "He never knew who he was." But who does? Who are you? Who am I? Is our name really not Legion? There are many selves within each of us. We hide behind many masks from one another. Sometimes our masks are peeled back like layers of skin on an onion and reveal so often that we are hollow at the center. Was T. S. Eliot correct? Are we merely "the hollow men, the stuffed men, leaning together, headpiece filled with straw?" Without a polestar, without a center of gravity, without knowledge of who we are, we are Legion—our nature is that of the demoniac.

We are, in Carl Sandburg's words, a menagerie. Within the wilderness inside each of us is a wolf, a fox, a hog, a fish, a baboon, an eagle, and other creatures. We are indeed paradoxical creatures. We are loving and hateful, harmful and saving, educating and destroying, wise and foolish, visionary and shortsighted. Each of us is the "Keeper of the Zoo." We may deny it, but we cannot hide it. There is a wilderness in every person. Here is the Legion element of our inner struggle which can be calmed only by the power and strength of the re-creative spirit of Christ. Listen to Jesus when he cried out to Legion, "Come out of him!" But Legion responded, "What have you to do with me, Jesus, Son of the Most High God?" He sounds like today's crowd. It is contemporary man's reaction to the Christ. What have you to do with me, Jesus Christ? Leave me undisturbed, unchanged, uncommitted, uninvolved. Before Christ can cast any evil spirit out of a person's life, he comes first as tormentor. He comes as disturber. When we are initially confronted by Christ, he comes in judgment. A single life standing in the light of the judgment of his presence sees the dimension of the wilderness within, the immensity of the force of Legion within, which divides and perplexes one's personality. He will not leave our prejudices unchallenged; our attitudes rigid; lesser values cannot remain when higher ones are possible; brokenness is molded into wholeness, depravity is overpowered by redeeming grace, the status quo is constantly moving toward renewal.

In *Brothers Karamazov* Dostoevski tells a striking tale of the return of Christ to Seville where he performs many wonderful acts of healing before he is arrested and thrown in prison by the Grand Inquisitor. Later the Grand Inquisitor confronts Jesus and inquires why he had to return at the present time and disturb the life and teachings of the church. Without a word Jesus accepts all the abuse that is directed at him. Finally without a comment Christ leans over and kisses the blood-drained lips of the religious leader. The Grand Inquisitor, unable to stand the presence of Christ, opens the prison door and shouts: "Go, and come no more! Come not at all, never, never!" Christ is the great disturber. No life can remain the same when confronted by his presence. Alfred North Whitehead once pictured our human reaction to the divine this way: "Religion is the transition from God the void to God the enemy, and from God the enemy to God the companion." First we pass through the door of Christ's judgment before he brings a center into our divided lives.

Legion's cry, then, was real, and it is the cry of every person: "What have you to do with me, Jesus, Son of the Most High God? I beseech you, do not torment me." But redemption did come to this disturbed man. His torn personality found wholeness through the power of Christ. "Come out of the man, you unclean spirit!" Here is the act of redemption, freeing a man's spirit from chaos to unity, conflict to peace, bondage to freedom, despair to hope, fragmentation to oneness. Jesus Christ offers to each of us the unification and integration of personality. He calls a truce to the internal civil war and furnishes wholeness and

217

stability. If Jesus' exorcism is viewed merely as a healing, the deep implications of the cosmic dimension of salvation is minimized. It is clear from the gospel accounts that Jesus wanted to avoid the reputation of simply being a healer. There was a cosmic element to his healings. The salvation of Jesus is concerned with the total person, not just the physical self, or the moral or spiritual side, but the whole person and his other interrelatedness. Redemption is concerned with overcoming everyone's estrangement from himself, others, and God.

The mighty contradiction which we sense in the universe goes beyond our need merely for redemption of individual sins, we experience the power of collective evil. The modern demons which threaten to destroy us are more than just the sum of individual evil acts. Exorcizing demons modern style will involve redeeming not only individuals but the systems which have enslaved them. The evil forces which crucified Christ are representative of the corporate aspect of evil. The collective evil which destroyed the life of Christ is ever present. Look at this evil: religious intolerance, commercial graft, political corruption, injustice, the mob mentality, public apathy, militarism, and the class system. These are evil forces deeply rooted within our social systems. Jesus was crucified by a system which allowed him to be executed although he was found innocent. As a member of the lower class he was not given representation or defense. But corporate evil is not confined to the first century. Confronting the collective power of evil is the modern equivalent of exorcising demons. The church, as Walter Rauschenbusch said over fifty years ago, is the social factor of salvation. The church is the social force in the world which challenges the collective powers of evil. At least it should be! The church, to use Harvey Cox's phrase, is "the cultural exorcist." The church is the social force which says, for example, that not only do we seek to challenge and overcome racial prejudice but we shall strive to help minority groups attain their own sense of personal respect and dignity.

Some voices say all we need to do is get persons to make a personal commitment to Christ and the problem with society will be solved. I wish it were so! In a community in the South a young minister attempted to relate the gospel to include persons of all races. He was told he could not enter the pulpit again, and he, his wife, and five children were put out of their home within a week. Was that church, where individuals had made "commitments" to Christ, free from the demonic power of evil? Deeper dimensions of redemption and healing were needed. Sometimes, instead of being the force to change society, the church is perpetuating the very evil from which it needs deliverance. But the challenge remains: the church is called today to be the exorcist, the healer, and the deliverer from the demonic forces in society.

Notice again the epilogue of the story. After the demoniac had received redemption, the townspeople did not respond very well. They were terrified by a man who had such powers, and seemed little concerned with the change in Legion. The owners of the pigs were also greatly disturbed at their loss. They appeared more upset about the loss of the pigs than the cure of the man. How contemporary can a story be! Pigs are more important than people, they are saying. Property rights are more important than human rights. The mirror is before us as we sense modern man's reaction to open housing, racial desegregation, poverty, and the ghettos. Property is more important than people. Here is a demonic force whose power is so intense that it is incessantly moving us closer to chaos. Cured and sane, Legion desired to follow Jesus. But Jesus instructed him to go to the toughest territory of all for him to demonstrate his wholeness—go home. Go home and show your family and friends the wholeness and unity which God has given you. No easy task for anyone.

T. H. White, in a modern fantasy entitled *The Sword and the Stone,* depicts a contest between Merlin the magician and the evil witch, Madame Mim. It is a contest to the death, each using his or her greatest skill and powers. Madame Mim assumes many horrible and deadly shapes, but each time Merlin meets her with one better until finally the witch is annihilated. Through the centuries evil has assumed many forms, shapes, and disguises. It has come in all kinds of clothing, manners, and descriptions. Sometimes it was recognized in the form of one nation enslaving another, or a small group of men crushing any in the way of their self-appointed goal, or one individual demanding absolute obedience to his fanatical wishes. Whatever shape evil may take, the Christian must never lose sight of the fact that he is indeed engaged in a conflict, "an unseen warfare," with the "principalities and powers." But the Christian engages in this struggle with the assurance of victory. Through Jesus Christ we find inner courage and strength, "having done all, to stand." The Christian is aware, though he or she may stumble under the impact of the demonic power, that ultimately evil will be defeated. In hope and anticipation, we shout in the face of evil the words from the Apostle Paul: "If God is on our side, who is against us? . . . And yet, in spite of all, overwhelming victory is ours through him who loved us. For I am convinced that there is nothing in death or life, in the realm of spirits or superhuman powers, in the world as it is or the world as it shall be, in the forces of the universe, in heights or depths—nothing in all creation that can separate us from the love of God in Christ Jesus our lord" (Rom. 8:31, 37-39 NEB).

NOTES

1. Cox, *The Secular City* (New York: Macmillan, 1965), p. 149.
2. Tillich, *The Eternal Now* (New York: Scribner's, 1963), p. 60.
3. Morris, *Mankind My Church* (Nashville: Abingdon Press, 1971), p. 11.

APPENDIX:
Guidelines
for Studying a Sermon

The following apparatus is the editor's adaptation of a scheme by Ozora S. Davis, as set forth in Davis' *Principles of Preaching*. It includes suggestions from Andrew W. Blackwood's *Protestant Pulpit*. In addition, it reflects some concerns of the editor and of two of his graduate students in homiletics, James M. Stinespring and James Mattison King.

In studying a sermon, these factors should be considered:

OVERALL IMPRESSION: Was the sermon interesting? Informative? Moving? Convincing?

ANALYSIS: Outline the sermon, giving main point and first subpoints. Include Introduction and Conclusion.

TITLE: Is it attractive? Clear? Honest? Related to main theme?

TEXT: Is there a single text, or are there multiple texts? Section, chapter, paragraph, sentence, phrase, or word? Used literally, analogically, typologically, or allegorically? Vitally related to sermon? Historical meaning accurately reflected?

CENTRAL IDEA: What is it? Is it formally stated? Where? Does sermon fulfill its promise?

INTRODUCTION: Does it seize attention at once? Relate theme or text to hearers? Is it too long? Too short? Irrelevant?

BODY: Are main points clearly stated? Related to central idea? A unity? Is there forward movement? Is each point given space according to its importance? Where is climax reached?

CONCLUSION: Does it summarize main points? Or reinforce main discussion? Or call for decision or action?

SUPPORTIVE MATERIAL:

Sources: *Percent*

Preacher's thought and experience

Bible

Biography

History and literature

Observation of contemporary life

*Types.** Restatement? Examples—general, specific, hypothetical? Illustrations—anecdotes, parables, figures of speech? Argument? Testimony?

Quality: Varied? Apt? Fresh? True? Accurate? Right length?

TRANSITIONS AND CONNECTIVES: Varied? Natural?

UNITY: Does the sermon give an overall impression of wholeness?

STYLE: Is the style literary or oral? Abstract or concrete? Clear? Precise? Energetic? Natural? Beautiful? Individual? Are sentences varied in length and form?

GENERAL OBSERVATIONS: Does this sermon present a positive message? Is there an unusual format? What other striking features did you note? Was the appeal rational, affectional, ethical, or a combination of two or three?

---

*Definitions and examples of these terms can be found in the editor's books: *Learning to Speak Effectively* (London: Hodder & Stoughton, 1966; Grand Rapids: Baker Book House, 1974) or *A Guide to Biblical Preaching* (Nashville: Abingdon, 1976).

Biographical Notes

ACHTEMEIER, ELIZABETH: Born in Bartlesville, Okla., 1926. Educated at Stanford Univ.; Union Theol. Sem.; Columbia, Heidelberg, and Basel Univs. Ordained min., United Ch. of Christ. Taught at Union Theol. Sem., N.Y., 1954-56. Visiting lect., Lancaster Theol. Sem., 1959-71; Gettysburg Luth. Theol. Sem., 1968. Adjunct prof., Lancaster Theol. Sem., 1971-73. Visiting prof., Pittsburgh Theol. Sem., 1976-77; Presb. Sch. of Christian Ed., 1979; Union Theol. Sem., Va., since 1973. Lectures and preaches frequently before church, college, and seminary groups throughout the U.S. Mrs. Achtemeier believes that "there is really no improvement which can be made on Paul's statement in I Corinthians 1:21: 'It pleased God through the folly of the message we preach to save those who believe.' God, in his incredible mercy, has chosen us preachers as the instrument through which he *works* among his gathered people in the church. Our message is the cross and the resurrection, and through that message God *acts* to forgive human beings, to make them into new creatures with new possibilities, to reconcile them to himself, and thereby to give them joy and hope and abundant and eternal life. That we should be the instrument of such divine activity is a fantastic gift—and a terrifying responsibility. To paraphrase Paul once again, 'Woe to us if we do not preach the Gospel!'" Her books include: *The Feminine Crisis in Christian Faith* (1965); *The Old Testament and the Proclamation of the Gospel* (1973); *The Committed Marriage* (1976); *Creative Preaching* (1980). Co-author with husband: *The Old Testament*

Roots of Our Faith (1962); *To Save All People* (1967); *Proclamation: Epiphany, Series C* (1973).

BURGHARDT, WALTER JOHN: Born in New York City, 1914. Educated at Woodstock Coll., Catholic Univ. of America. Ordained priest, Roman Catholic Ch. Prof. of Patristic Theol., Woodstock Coll., 1946–. Biweekly radio program WWIN, Baltimore, Md., 1961-69. Pres., Mariological Soc. of Am., 1960-62. Pres., Patristic Acad. of Am., 1958–. Mariological Award for 1958. Honorary degrees: Univ. of Notre Dame, Univ. of Scranton. Fr. Burghardt preaches from a conviction of the power of words. While strongly committed to the significance of the sacraments, he believes that "the peril of liturgy is that it can be impersonal. The homily personalizes what the rite expresses in a common and general way. It should rouse the faith of this people more personally than is possible for liturgical symbols and ritual actions." Thus he consumes four hours in preparation for every minute in the pulpit. His books include: *The Idea of Catholicism* (1960); *All Lost in Wonder: Sermons of Theology and Life* (1960); *Saints and Sanctity* (1965); *Tell the Next Generation: Homilies and Near Homilies* (1980).

CLAYPOOL, JOHN ROWAN: Born in Franklin, Ky., 1930. Educated at Mars Hill Jr. Coll.; Baylor Univ.; So. Bapt. Theol. Sem. A Baptist. Pastor: Gilead Bapt. Ch., Richmond, Ky., 1952-55; First Bapt. Ch., Hartsville, Tenn., 1957-59; Asst. Pastor, First Bapt. Ch., Decatur, Ga., 1959-60; Pastor, Crescent Hill Bapt. Ch., Louisville, Ky., 1960-71; Broadway Bapt. Ch., Ft. Worth, Tex., 1971-76; Northminster Bapt. Ch., Jackson, Miss., 1976–. Chmn. Christian Life Comm., So. Bapt. Conv., 1963-64; member, Human Relations Comm., City of Ft. Worth. Named Young Man of Yr. in Religion, Louisville Jaycees, 1965. A notable characteristic of Claypool's preaching is his "confessional" approach, that is, his stating of a problem in terms of the way it is affecting him and the way he is having to struggle with it. He believes that he can touch other people who are struggling with the same problems and often motivate them to deal with them. "The confessional approach to problems," he says, "takes some of the shame and loneliness out of the difficulty." Books: *Tracks of a Fellow Struggler* (1974); *Stages: The Art of Living the Expected* (1977); *The Preaching Event* (1980), which comprises his Lyman Beecher Lectures at Yale.

COFFIN, WILLIAM SLOANE: Born in New York City, 1924. Educated at Phillips Acad.; Yale Sch. of Mus.; Union Theol. Sem.; Yale Univ. A Presbyterian. Service with CIA, 1950-53. Acting chaplain, Phillips Acad., 1956-57. Chaplain, Williams Coll., 1957-58; Yale Univ., 1958-75. Senior min., Riverside Ch., New York City, since 1977. Memb. of several boards of directors, incl. Pres.'s Advisory Council Peace Corps, Operation Crossroads Afr., Am. Freedom of Residence Fund. Coffin has been and is an outspoken activist in matters of social concern, whether of local or internatl. scope. The sermon included here was preached before a Christmas visit with the American hostages in the U.S. Embassy in Iran. He is the author of *Once to Every Man* (1977), an autobiography.

COX, JAMES WILLIAM: Born in Kingston, Tenn., 1923. Educated at Carson-Newman Coll.; So. Bapt. Theol. Sem.; Union Theol. Sem.; Princeton Theol. Sem.; Univ. of Zurich; Internatl. Bapt. Sem., Rüschlikon, Switzerland; Harvard Univ. Pastor: Nance's Grove Bapt. Ch., New Market, Tenn., 1943-44; Memorial Bapt. Ch., Frankfort, Ky., 1945-53; Central Bapt. Ch., Johnson City, Tenn., 1954-59. Visiting lect., Princeton Theol. Sem., 1964-65; Protestant Episcopal Sem., Alexandria, Va., 1977. Prof. of Christian Preaching, So. Bapt. Theol. Sem., 1959–. Lecturer and preacher, Natl. Preaching Clinic, Dayton, Ohio, 1978. Pres., Acad. of Homiletics, 1976-77. Contributing Ed., *The Pulpit Digest*, 1973–. Cox believes that preaching involves basic mechanics of structure, style, and delivery that are like those of other types of speech, but that there are distinctive qualities of rationale, content, and function that set the sermon apart from every other type of speech. Biblical preaching is to be preferred because the Bible provides a wide variety of interesting material, common ground with the hearer, and effective authority. More definitely than is true of topical opinion-sharing, preaching that takes the Bible text seriously often becomes "the catalyst of a divine-human encounter." Auth., *Learning to Speak Effectively* (1966, 1974); *A Guide to Biblical Preaching* (1976); *Surprised by God* (1979). Ed., *The Twentieth Century Pulpit* (1978). Co-comp., with Ernest A. Payne and Stephen F. Winward, *Minister's Worship Manual* (1969). Co-auth. with Eduard Schweizer and trans., *God's Inescapable Nearness* (1971).

CRADDOCK, FRED B.: Born in Humboldt, Tenn., 1928. Educated at Johnson Bible Coll.; Phillips, Vanderbilt, Tübingen, and Yale Univs. Member, Disciples of Christ. Served pastorates in Tenn. and Okla. Taught at Phillips Univ. 1961-79; Candler Sch. of Theol. 1979–. Mem. Gen. Board and Adm. Comm. of the Christian Church; Comm. on Theol. of the Council on Christian Unity. Numerous lectureships, including Lyman Beecher Lectures at Yale. He has emphasized the importance of an inductive approach in preaching, believing that present-day hearers are more receptive to truth when it is presented indirectly. In his research in the writings of Kierkegaard he has found confirmation of the special significance of "overhearing the gospel." His books include: *As One Without Authority* (1971, rev. 1974) and *Overhearing the Gospel* (1978).

CRUM, MILTON, JR.: Born in Orangeburg, S.C., 1924. Educated at Clemson Univ.; Univ. of Neb.; Univ. of the South Sch. of Theol.; Wesley Theol. Sem.; Luth. Theol. So. Sem.; St. Augustine's Coll. (Canterbury, Eng.). An Episcopalian. Rector, Ch. of the Holy Communion, Allendale, S.C., 1951-60. Episcopal chaplain, Clemson Univ., 1960-66. Prof. of homiletics, Episcopal Theol. Sem. in Va., since 1966. Crum writes: "A sermon which moves from an area of life standing in need of the gospel to that area of life as transformed by the gospel has the basic characteristics of a story. A human story begins somewhere in human life and moves somewhere, and the movement makes a significant difference. Such a sermon, like any story, will include (1) verbal content, (2) a structure, and (3) a dynamic." Thus the sermon could naturally take the form of situation, complication, and resolution, whether based on a narrative incident or a didactic text. In elaborating such a structure, these dynamic factors will come into play: (1) certain symptomatic behavior, (2) the root of that behavior, (3) the unhappy consequences, (4) the gospel content needed to produce change of mind and heart *and* behavior, and (5) the new results that follow the new way of believing and perceiving provided by the gospel. He has written numerous articles and a book, *Manual on Preaching* (1977).

DAVIES, ELAM: Born in Grovesend, Swansea, Wales, in 1916. Educated at Univ. of Wales and Cambridge (Eng.) Univ. A Presbyterian. Min. in Wales, 1944-52; Bethlehem, Pa., 1952-61; Fourth Presb. Ch., Chicago, since 1961. Taught philos. theol. and Christian ethics, Temple Univ., 1953-55. Mem. of board of managers, central dept. of evangelism, Natl. Council of Chs., 1956-66. Mem. of numerous other important boards and committees. Cited by *Time* (1980) as one of seven American star preachers, Davies is "a consummate, self-conscious and often florid dramatist of the pulpit. . . . As a preacher, he tries to translate the Gospel into the idiom of today, so that 'the Bible comes alive and the Christian faith is made believable.'" Author of *This Side of Eden* (sermons, 1964).

FORD, D. W. CLEVERLEY: Born in Sheringham, Eng., 1914. Educated at Univ. of London. An Anglican. Tutor, London Coll. of Div., 1936–39; Curate in Bridlington, Eng., 1934-42. Vicar, Hampstead, London, 1942-55; Kensington Gore, 1955-74. Senior chaplain to Archbishop of Canterbury, 1975–. Dir., Coll. of Preachers, 1960-73. Chaplain to Queen Elizabeth II, 1973–. He believes that preaching stands in a class by itself and that "the formidable obstacles preaching has to face in the modern world" cannot invalidate it. Preaching, therefore, while similar to other forms of address which are being criticized or ignored, goes its own way to accomplish what it was intended to do. He says: "A preacher in the last resort only has authority if he is a *man of God*. . . . When such a man of God speaks there is nothing you can say or do except listen." In fulfilling his own ministry, Ford has labored hard to couch his thoughts in clear, simple, concrete language. The wide reception of his books testifies to his success. He has written many books on preaching, including: *An Expository Preacher's Notebook* (1960); *A Theological Preacher's Notebook* (1962); *A Pastoral Preacher's Notebook* (1965); *Preaching Today* (1969); *Preaching through the Christian Year* (1971); *New Preaching from the Old Testament* (1976); *New Preaching from the New Testament* (1977); *The Ministry of the Word* (1979). His autobiography: *Have You Anything to Declare?* (1973).

FRY, JOHN R.: Born in Van Buren, Ark., 1923. Educated at Colgate Univ. and Union Theol. Sem. A Presbyterian. Pastor, Blue Ash Presb. Ch., 1952-56. Ed., Board of Christian Ed., Presb. Ch., U.S.A., 1956-60. News ed., *Presbyterian Life* mag., 1960-65. Pastor, First Presb. Ch., Chicago, 1965-71. Visiting prof., San Francisco Theol. Sem., 1971-73; Graduate Theol. Union, 1973-75. Ed. with his wife, Carl Alice, of *Frying Pan,* a mag. of theological/social commentary. In 1969 Fry said, "The time for great preaching of great sermons to great churches is over." With such a conviction, he preached "non-sermons." In the context in which he served, he did not find time to consider reflectively the problem of preaching. "Typically," he wrote, "a thirteen- or fourteen-page handwritten sermon manuscript was prepared on Saturday night. Sometimes the entire Saturday night. This meant that the selection of a Biblical text, done sometime earlier in the week, was all that had been done. Exegesis, thought, theological work, preparation, and writing had to be telescoped into simultaneous operations. . . . Preaching

. . . was forced to be flat out because that was the style of the church." Author of numerous magazine articles. Has lectured and preached at many colleges, universities, and theological schools. His books include: *The Immobilized Christian* (1963); *Fire and Blackstone* (sermons, etc., 1969); *The Locked Out Americans* (1973).

GLADSTONE, JOHN: Born in London, Eng., 1921. Educated at Manchester Bapt. Coll., Manchester Univ. A Baptist. Min. of churches in Eng.: in Reading, Plymouth, and Kent. Min. of Yorkminster Park Bapt. Ch., Toronto, Canada since 1965. From 1940-45 he served in the Royal Air Force. He conducted preaching missions in several countries. Gladstone strongly affirms the significance of preaching: "We have a magnificent Faith, a glorious Gospel, and although I am often ashamed of the preacher, I am never ashamed of my calling to communicate what God has so graciously given! . . . I know of no more exhilarating task than that of lifting up Christ in the fullness of His stature, His saving power and His costly demands." The author of two vols. of sermons: *The Valley of the Verdict* (1968); *A Magnificent Faith* (1979).

GOMES, PETER JOHN: Born in Boston, Mass., 1942. Educated at Bates Coll. and Harvard Div. Sch. Baptist. Dir., Freshmen Program, Tuskeegee (Ala.) Inst., 1968-70. Asst. min., Harvard Memorial Ch., Cambridge, Mass., 1970-72; acting min., 1972-74; min. and Plummer prof. of Christian Morals at the univ., 1974–. Mem. of several boards of trustees and learned societies. Recognized in 1980 by *Time* as one of the outstanding preachers in the U.S. His sermons are marked by a combination of biblical scholarship and timely application, clarity and appropriate humor. Author of *History of the Pilgrim Society, 1820-1970* (1971). Editor of *History of the Town of Plymouth, James Thacker, 1835* (1972); *Theology and Literature of the Pilgrims* (1975).

HULL, WILLIAM E.: Born in Birmingham, Ala., 1930. Educated at Univ. of Alabama; Samford Univ.; So. Bapt.

Theol. Sem.; Univ. of Göttingen, Germany; and Harvard Univ. A Baptist. Taught at So. Bapt. Theol. Sem., 1955-75. Dean, Sch. of Theol., 1969-75; Provost, 1972-75. Pastor: Beulah Bapt. Ch., Wetumpka, Ala., 1950-51; Cedar Hill Bapt. Ch., Owenton, Ky., 1952-53; First Bapt. Ch., New Castle, Ky., 1953-58; First Bapt. Ch., Shreveport, La., since 1975. Speaker at numerous conventions and conferences. Lect. for several distinguished lectureships. Hull says of the sermon included here that it was born out of pastoral travail and has ministered very directly to what he calls his own prayer poverty as well as to the needs of others. His sermons attempt to translate faithfully into a timely message the historical affirmations of Scripture. He says, "It is urgent that the Bible be used in such a way that it will speak unmistakably to the Church, even when the Church does not care to listen!" Author of "John," *Broadman Bible Commentary,* vol. 9 (1970); *The Bible* (1974). Contrib.: *Professor in the Pulpit* (1963); *The Truth That Makes Men Free* (1966); *Salvation in Our Time* (1978).

KIVENGERE, FESTO: Born in Kigezi District, Uganda, East Afr., 1920. Educated at Bishop Tucker Coll., Uganda; Univ. of London; Pittsburgh Theol. Sem. An Anglican. Teacher in Kabale, Uganda, 1940-45. Teacher and evangelist, Central Tanzania, 1946-59. School supervisor, Kigezi District, Uganda, 1960-62. Freelance evangelist, 1953-71. Bishop of Kigezi Diocese, Western Uganda, 1972–. Recipient of Internatl. Freedom Prize, Oslo, Norway, 1977. His preaching is kindled with the fire of the first post-Easter Pentecost and is done with the conviction that God's love can win out in even the most difficult circumstances. He gave the message included here in Lausanne at the International Congress on World Evangelization in 1974, when political, economic, and religious conditions were becoming increasingly fearful in his native Uganda. His writings include: *When God Moves in Revival* (1973); *Love Unlimited* (1975); *I Love Idi Amin* (1977); *The Spirit Is Moving* (1979).

MASSEY, JAMES EARL: Born in Ferndale, Mich., 1930. Educated at Detroit Con. of Music; Univ. of Detroit; Salzburg Mozarteum, Austria; Detroit Bible Coll.; Oberlin Coll.; Univ. of Mich.; Pacific Sch. of Rel. Member of Ch. of God (Anderson, Ind.). Assoc. pastor, Ch. of God of Detroit, 1953-54; founder and senior pastor, Metropolitan Ch. of God, Detroit, 1954-76. On leave from pastorate, pres. of Jamaica Sch. of Theol. in Kingston, 1963-66. Since 1969 he has taught as a prof. of homiletics and worship at Anderson Grad. Sch. of Theol. Since 1977, regular speaker on Christian Brotherhood Hour, an international weekly broadcast on over 400 radio stations. Delegate to several world religious conventions. Mem. of numerous organizations and boards. His sermons are characterized by evangelical warmth, theological insight, and exegetical thoroughness. They are couched in graphic language in an easily understood style. Among his twelve books in the field of religions are two on preaching: *The Sermon in Perspective* (1976) and *Designing the Sermon* (1980).

MOLTMANN, JÜRGEN: Born in Hamburg, Germany, in 1926. Educated at Univ. of Göttingen. Mem. of the Reformed Ch. Pastor for five years at Bremen. Taught at Univ. of Göttingen; Kirchlichehochschule, Wuppertal; Univ. of Bonn; Univ. of Tübingen since 1967; Duke Univ. (guest prof.), 1967-68. He writes: "The 'event' of the sermon is the living person of the liberator Jesus Christ. In him comes the joy of God to an otherwise often joyless world. Through him fall the chains which often make men sad and angry. . . . According to my conviction, scholarly theology has for its target the sermon just as every recognition of truth aims at a practice which will change false reality. . . . Though not the only means, the sermon is one of the best for liberating the internally and externally oppressed man for faith, love and hope." His books in Eng. trans. include: *Theology of Hope* (1967): *The Future of Hope* (1970); *The Gospel of Liberation* (sermons, 1973); *The Experiment Hope* (1975); *The Future of Creation* (1979); *Hope for the Church* (1979).

MYERS, JEAN: Born in Washington, D.C., 1956. Educated at the Coll. of William and Mary; So. Bapt. Theol. Sem. A Baptist. Mem. of Kappa Delta Pi, Natl. honor soc. for education. Employed by several firms as clerk-typist, 1973-77. She is currently a candidate for the M.Div. degree. "Naked, but Not Ashamed" is her first sermon and is the only sermon by a student for the ministry in this collection. It was presented in a class made up of ministerial students. It was delivered with poise and conviction and without manuscript or notes. It was impressive both for its subject matter and for its delivery.

NAPIER, B. DAVIE: Born in Kuling, China, 1915. Educated at Samford Univ.; Yale Univ.; Wesleyan Univ. Taught at: Judson Coll., 1939-40; Alfred Univ., 1944-46; Univ. of Ga., 1946-49; Yale Univ., 1949-56; 1964-66. Dean of the Chapel, Stanford Univ., 1966-72. Pres. of the Pacific Sch. of Rel., Berkeley, Cal., 1972-77; Dean of the College Chapel at Mount Holyoke Coll., South Hadley, Mass., 1977-80; now master of Calhoun Coll. and a prof. in the div. sch. at Yale. In 1975, he gave the Lyman Beecher Lectures at Yale. Napier said, in the Beecher Lectures, "I do not see how contemporary ministry, particularly on the ancient prophetic model, can be faithful either to the Word of God or the word of earth except as it is lived and preached in a sense of God and of earth—must be heard and proclaimed simultaneously." Books: *Come Sweet Death* (1967); *Time of Burning* (1970); *Word of God, Word of Earth* (1976).

PARRENT, ALLAN MITCHELL: Born in Frankfort, Ky., 1930. Educated at Georgetown Coll., Ky.; Vanderbilt, Duke, and Durham (Eng.) Univs. An Episcopalian layman. Fellowships: Danforth Grad. Fellow; Rockefeller Theol. Fellow; Falk Fellow; Gurney Harris Kearns Fellow in Rel. Served as Foreign Service Officer, U.S. Dept. of State, 1962-64. Member of U.S. Delegation to the Eighteen-Nation Disarmament Conf., Geneva, 1964. Asst. coord. of student activities and asst. dir. of the student union, Duke Univ., 1964-67. Dir. of Program in Wash.,

Dept. of Internatl. Affairs, Natl. Council of Chs., 1967-72.
Prof. of Ch. and Soc., Protestant Episcopal Theol. Sem. in
Va., 1972–. Recitalist, Young Artist's Concert Assoc.,
1954-55. Tenor soloist with numerous groups. Recordings
with the Camerata Chorus of Wash. Co-chairman, Am.
Comm., Council on Christian Approaches to Defense and
Disarmament. Mem.: Comm. of the Dept. of Internatl.
Affairs, Natl. Council of Chs.; Internatl. Inst. for Strategic
Studies; Arms Control Assoc. Author of numerous journal
articles. He views his sermon printed here "as an effort to
integrate theology with the total work of the 'laos' in that
world which God in Christ creates, preserves, and
redeems." He believes that sermons "can be part of the
glue that properly binds together what God never intended
to be put asunder . . . , i.e., 'Christianity' and 'real life.'"
Other publications: *The Problem of the Anti-ballistic
Missile* (1967); *War Crimes: U.S. Priorities and Military
Force* (1972); *The Responsible Use of Power: The Cuban
Missile Crisis in Christian Perspective* (unpub. Ph.D. diss.,
1969).

RICE, CHARLES L.: Born in Chandler, Okla., 1936.
Educated at Baylor Univ.; So. Bapt. Theol. Sem.; Union
Theol. Sem.; Duke Univ. Minister of United Ch. of Christ.
Pastor, Chapel Hill, N.C., 1967-68; Durham, N.C., 1970.
Taught at: Div. Sch., Duke Univ., 1963-67; Salem Coll.,
1967-68; Federal Theol. Sem., Alice So. Afr., 1968; Theol.
and Grad. Schls., Drew Univ., since 1970. Adjunct prof.,
Princeton Theol. Sem. and Union Theol. Sem., 1975-76.
Voight lect. at McKendree Coll., 1976. Editor of *Word and
Witness*. Rice believes (with Morris Niedenthal) that "the
formative image that could articulate what preaching is and
free people to do it" is *story*. "At the most profound level of
symbolization—where experience becomes meaningful—
we relate our stories to The Story. If we were pressed to say
what Christian faith and life are, we could hardly do better
than *hearing, telling, and living a story*. And if asked for a
short definition of preaching could we do better than *shared
story?*" Books: *Interpretation and Imagination: The Preacher*

and Contemporary Literature (1970); (with J. Louis Martyn) *Proclamation: Aids for Interpreting the Lessons of the Church Year* (1975); (with Edmund A. Steimle and Morris Niedenthal) *Preaching the Story* (1980).

ROBINSON, JOHN A. T.: Born in Canterbury, Kent, Eng., 1919. Educated at Marlborough Coll.; Jesus Coll.; Trinity Coll.; and Westcott House, Cambridge Univ. An Anglican. Curate, Bristol, Eng., 1945-48. Chaplain and lect., Wells Theol. Coll., Wells, Eng., 1948-51. Fellow and dean of Clare Coll., Cambridge Univ., 1951-59. Univ. lect. in div., 1953-59. Bishop of Wollwich, Ch. of England, Diocese of Southwark, 1959-69; asst. bishop since 1969. Examining Chaplain to Archbishop of Canterbury, 1953-58. Visiting prof., Harvard Univ., 1955; Union Theol. Sem., Richmond, Va., 1958; Univ. of So. Afr., Pretoria, 1975; Univ. of Witwatersrand, 1977. Six Preacher, Canterbury Cathedral, 1958-63. Lect. in Theol., Fellow, and Dean of Chapel, Trinity Coll., Cambridge, since 1959. Referring to the sermon in this book, Robinson says: "I am inclined . . . to think that its theme is probably the most central one that Christian theology has currently to come to terms with, avoiding both an exclusivist triumphalism on the one hand and a helpless syncretism on the other. I want to see a strong centre with open edges rather than a soft centre with hard edges." Books: *The Body* (1952); *Liturgy Coming to Life* (1960); *Honest to God* (1963); *But That I Can't Believe* (1967); *The Human Face of God* (1973); *Redating the New Testament* (1977); *Truth Is Two-Eyed* (1979); *The Roots of a Radical* (1980). Trans.: *The New English Bible.* Contrib.: *The Interpreter's Dictionary of the Bible.*

SCHULLER, ROBERT H.: Born in Alton, Iowa, in 1926. Educated at Hope Coll. and Western Theol. Sem. Min. of the Reformed Ch. in America. Pastor, Ivanhoe Reformed Ch., Chicago, 1950-55; Garden Grove (Cal.) Comm. Ch., 1955-. Began his West Coast ministry in a drive-in theater. Has led in building two church plants; the latter, the "Crystal Cathedral," with 10,000 windows and 4,000 seats, cost above $15 million. The Morning worship, called *The Hour of Power,* is telecast on about 200 stations in North America, Australia, and New Zealand, as well as on the Armed Forces network, to an audience of three million. Schuller's sermons emphasize "possibility thinking." He avoids theological jargon, attempting to state a positive message "in a practical manner and in helpful human terms." He asks critics who question his message of possibility thinking, "What is the alternative?" His many books include: *God's Way to the Good Life* (1963); *You Can Become the Person You Want to Be* (1973); and *Peace of Mind Through Possibility Thinking* (1977).

STASSEN, GLEN H.: Born in St. Paul, Minn., 1936. Educated at Univ. of Va.; Union Theol. Sem., N.Y.; Duke Univ.; Harvard Univ. A Baptist. Taught at: Duke Univ., 1963-64; Ky. So. Coll., 1964-69; Berea Coll. 1972-76; So. Bapt. Theol. Sem. since 1976. Has been a minister in churches in Ky., Va., and Penn. Fellowships at Harvard Univ.: Harvard Center for Internatl. Affairs Research Fellow, 1971-72; Soc. for Rel. in Higher Ed. Cross-Disciplinary Fellowship, 1970-71; Natl. Endowment for the Humanities Younger Scholar Fellowship, 1969-70. Duke Univ.: Gurney Harris Kearns Fellowship, 1962-73; Duke Univ. Grad. Fellowship, 1961-62; Lilly Fellowship, 1960-61. God's delivering love is central in Stassen's ethics. His aim in preaching is to help people to allow a breakthrough in their pre-understandings of what the Scriptures are trying to say. He believes the repression of the unpleasantness of nuclear war, and the reduction of the Sermon on the Mount to a limited ideal or a narrow prohibition, prevent people from seeing the surprising initiatives suggested by God's delivering love, and the resultant realistic hope. He is the author of numerous articles in scholarly and professional journals, and has contributed chapters to the following books: *Power and Empowerment in Higher Education* (1978); *Issues and Values* (1975); *Issues in Christian Ethics* (1980).

THOMPSON, WILLIAM D.: Born in Chicago, Ill., 1929. Educated at Wheaton Coll.; No. Bapt. Theol. Sem.; Northwestern Univ.; Cambridge (Eng.) Univ. A Baptist. Pastor, Raymond Bapt. Ch., Chicago, 1956-58. Taught at No. Bapt. Theol. Sem., 1958-62; Eastern Bapt. Theol. Sem. since 1962. Faculty fellow, Am. Assn. Theol. Schs., 1968-69. Pres., Am. Acad. of Homiletics. Former ed. of *Preaching Today,* an ecumenical preaching journal. In his preaching Thompson attempts "to involve listeners at a visceral, existential level. The allusions are concrete, image-evoking. . . . People respond to the gospel," he believes, "when the preaching they hear deals at a gut level with those experiences." Author of *A Listener's Guide to Preaching* (1966); (with William Toohey) *Recent Homiletical Thought* (1967); (with Gordon C. Bennett) *Dialogue Preaching* (1969): General ed. for *Abingdon Preacher's Library,* a 10-vol. series being published in 1980-81.

TILLICH, PAUL JOHANNES: Born in Starzeddel, Kreis Guben, Germany, in 1886; died in 1965. Educated at Berlin, Tübingen, Breslau, and Halle Univs. Ordained min., Evang. Luth. Ch.; later mem. of United Ch. of Christ. Taught at Univ. of Berlin, 1919-24; Univs. of Marburg, Leipzig, and Frankfurt, 1924-33; Union Theol. Sem., New York, 1933-55; Harvard Univ., 1955-62; Univ. of Chicago Div. Sch., 1962-65. Recipient of numerous awards and honorary degrees. Author of a three-vol. work in systematic theology. Wilhelm Pauck comments: "His preaching style was marked by vivid example, concrete analogy, and such keen psychological perception that individual listeners often felt that the sermon was addressed specifically to them. . . . His message was not couched in abstract language but in meditatively poetic or psychological terms." His sermon "You Are Accepted," which "translates" the doctrine of justification by faith, was said to be Tillich's favorite. Author of three sermon vols.: *The Shaking of the Foundations* (1948); *The New Being* (1955);

The Eternal Now (1963). Biographical studies on Tillich were written by Rollo May, *Paulus* (1973); Hannah Tillich, *From Time to Time* (1973); and Wilhelm and Marion Pauck, *Paul Tillich: His Life and Thought,* vol. 1, (1976).

TING, K. H. (Ding Guangxun): Born in Shanghai, China, 1915. Educated at St. John's Univ., Shanghai; Columbia Univ. An Anglican. Student YMCA Secretary, Shanghai, 1938-43. Pastor, Internatl. Ch., Shanghai, 1943-46. Secretary, Student Christian Movement of Canada, 1946-47; World Student Christian Fed., 1948-51. In 1955, he was consecrated Bishop of Chekiang. From 1953, he has served as Principal of Nanking Theol. Coll. Recent positions held: Vice-chmn., Natl. Comm. of Chinese Christians for Promoting Self-Govt., Self-Support and Self-Propagation; Deputy to Natl. Peoples Congress, China; Vice-Chmn., Provincial Peoples Pol. Consultative Conf. of Kiangsu; Mem., Standing Comm., Natl. Peoples Consultative Conf. of China; Prof. and Dir., Centre for Rel. Studies, Nanking Univ. The sermon included here was delivered at Timothy Eaton Memorial Ch. in Toronto, Nov. 4, 1979.

TUCK, WILLIAM P.: Born in Lynchburg, Va., in 1934. Educated at Bluefield Jr. Coll., Univ. of Richmond, Southeastern Bapt. Theol. Sem., New Orleans Bapt. Theol. Sem., Emory Univ. A Baptist. Pastor of Good Hope Baptist Ch., Madison, Va., 1955-60; Calvary Bapt. Ch., Slidell, La., 1963-66; Harrisonburg Bapt. Ch., Harrisonburg, Va., 1966-69; First Bapt. Ch., Bristol, Va., 1969-78. Assoc. prof. of preaching, So. Bapt. Theol. Sem. since 1978. Has held numerous civic and professional chairmanships. Author of numerous articles on religious themes. In response to a query as to his preaching methods, Tuck has said: "I attempt to relate biblical and theological concepts in down-to-earth, practical, understandable images for contemporary persons. I draw freely on illustrative and pictorial images to communicate my thought. I prepare my sermons carefully but always preach extemporaneously without use of manuscript or notes." His books include, *Facing Grief and Death* (1975); *Knowing God: Religious Knowledge in the Theology of John Baillie* (1978); Ed. and contrib., *The Struggle for Meaning* (1977).